Gen Z 360

Hana Ben-Shabat

Gen Z 360

Preparing for the Inevitable Change in

Culture, Work, and Commerce

Z

First published in the United States in 2021 by Gen Z Planet, LLC

gen Z planet

www.genzplanet.com

Library of Congress Control Number: 2021902182

ISBN: 978-1-7347204-0-2
ISBN e-Book: 978-1-7347204-1-9

21 22 23 24 25 LSC 10 9 8 7 6 5 4 3 2 1

To my parents
Rachel and Isaac Ben-Shabat
with deep gratitude for your love, support,
and for everything I learned from you.

CONTENTS

ACKNOWLEDGMENTS

I HAVE ALWAYS wanted to write a book. And when I say "always," I mean it. The first time I had an idea for a book I was in sixth grade. Since then, through life and work, many ideas popped up and died off until this one, because this time it was no longer just about "a book." *Gen Z 360* means a lot to me personally. It is much more than a portrait of a generation or a set of recommendations about how to work with or market to Gen Z. It is a reflection of my passion and commitment to making a contribution, even a small one, to support the integration of the next generation into business and society in general.

I embarked on this book journey a couple of years ago and learned a lot along the way. Not surprisingly, I learned that behind every book and every author is an entire community of people who make a book happen, and I am thankful to all the people who became part of this project.

My "community" included first and foremost a panel of twenty Gen Zers who gave me an opportunity to get to know them and learn about their lives, their hobbies, their concerns, and their hopes for the future. I am grateful for their participation and for the open conversations we had.

A sincere thank you must go to the professors and lecturers who shared with me their research, points of view, and firsthand experience with their Gen Z students: David Schmid, Kathy Merlock Jackson, Shay Rahm, David Yaffe, Wendong Li, and Stan Silverman. Your insights and observations are greatly appreciated.

A special thank you goes to Florence Breslin of the Laureate Institute for Brain Research for sharing with me the initial findings of the Adolescent Brain Cognitive Development Study (ABCD), one of the most fascinating studies on brain development and child health, and to Trace Pickering for sharing the story and vision of the Iowa BIG school program. In addition, I am grateful to psychologists Angel Hu and Michael Minervini for their thoughtful contributions.

To the executives who shared with me their views about Gen Z and the future of work and commerce, thank you for being so generous with your time and for sharing your vision for the future: Maeve Coburn (L'Oréal), Barbra Katz (Crum & Forster), Krista Davis (Novartis), Daniel Jackson (Crestron), Daniel Robison (Loblaw), Christine Waddick (Sun Life Canada), Dennis Shuler (Kinetic Consulting), Matthew Komos (TransUnion), J. Allen Seelenbinder (Bank of America), Davide Bolis (4EON), and Julien Bouzitat (Amorepacific).

I am especially thankful to all the entrepreneurs who are building the companies and platforms of the future with Gen Z in mind. Your commitment to doing something different is truly inspiring, and I am fortunate to have had the opportunity to learn about your ventures: Nathan Candaner (JobzMall), Dean Brauer (gohenry), Gin Gindre (Rebellion), Marcel van Oost (M), Jennifer Barrett (Acorns), Tiffany Zhong (Zebra IQ), Annie Fong (Takumi), Brandon Leibel (Sand Cloud), Maria Raga (Depop), Tal Zvi Nathanel (Showfields), Neha Singh (Obsess), Rob Smith (The Phluid Project), Fabian Seelbach (Curology), and Zach Schwitzky (Limbik).

In addition, I would like to thank my "book team": Thomas Lee, for helping me to kickstart this project and for the editorial support given to the first and second parts of this book; Catherine Oliver for her diligent review of the manuscript and for the carefully considered recommendations she made. A special acknowledgment must go to John Paine for the constructive feedback he gave me throughout the editing rounds and for helping me to bring this project to the finish line. Thank you to Glen Edelstein of Hudson Valley Book Design for his patience and creativity, to Diane Kraut for her help with the permissions process, to Martin Schneider for his diligent proofreading, and to Laura Ogar for the rapid creation of the index.

To Sharonna Karni Cohen—founder of Dreame, a co-creation art platform—thank you for giving me access to Dreame's artists who made a few of the illustrations in this book. I am truly indebted to them and to all the other artists from around the world who joined this project and helped turn Gen Z's dreams into an artistic reality: Tatiana Boiko, Alfonso Cirillo, Jasmijn Evans, Victoria Fernandez, Francisco Fonseca, Betsy Huizi, Alex Krugli, Jaen Lassalle, Jone Leal, Selma Nached, Tayfun Pekdemir, Giovani Ramos, Maja Tomljanovic, Bea Vaquero, and Xuetong Wang. Your creativity and collaborative spirit are truly amazing. It was a great pleasure to work with all of you.

Finally, I want to thank my family and friends for their support and encouragement. This project has had its ups and downs and having you through it all made a big difference. To Arik and Roy, my Gen Z nephews, thank you for sharing your views on various topics and for the joy you bring to our family. Last but not least, to my best friend Mike—I am forever grateful for your friendship, kindness, honest feedback, and for challenging me every day to do better. This book would not have happened without your support.

—Hana Ben-Shabat
New York, January 2021

INTRODUCTION

IN JANUARY 2019, a teenage girl sporting purple pants, two long braids, and a deep, penetrating stare sat on a stage in front of the world's most powerful people—and made them squirm. "I don't want your hope," she said. "I want you to panic."[1]

Her name is Greta Thunberg, and at only 16 years old she has emerged as one of the world's most prominent activists on climate change. She had traveled by train to Davos, Switzerland, for the annual World Economic Forum, but rather than take selfies with celebrities and other bigwigs, the young Swede shamed them into silence.

Later that week, she spoke at an event hosted by Salesforce CEO Marc Benioff that included rock star Bono, scientist Jane Goodall, and an array of corporate executives and investors. "Some people say that the climate crisis is something that we all have created, but that is not true, because if everyone is guilty, then no one is to blame, and someone is to blame." She said, "Some people, some companies, some decision-makers, in particular, have known exactly what priceless values they have been sacrificing to continue making unimaginable amounts of money. And I think many of you here today belong to that group of people."[2]

A year later, in January 2020, Greta, who started her activist journey sitting alone in front of the Swedish government building, holding a sign saying "School Strike for Climate," was no longer alone. In the year that had passed, she had inspired and mobilized millions of teens around the world to strike for action around climate change. She returned to Davos to remind world leaders that they had not made enough progress.

Thunberg certainly speaks with conviction and maturity beyond her years. But she is hardly alone.

Twenty-one-year-old Emma Gonzalez, a survivor of the 2018 high school shooting in Parkland, Florida, has become a powerful proponent of gun control. "Since the time of the Founding Fathers and since they added the Second Amendment to the Constitution, our guns have developed at a rate that leaves me dizzy," Gonzales said in a rally held after the massacre. "The guns have changed, but our laws have not."[3] Her words inspired more than a million people to join the March for Our Lives on March 24, 2018. With a central event in Washington, D.C., and more than 800 related events across the United States and around the world,[4] the march was one of the largest youth-led demonstrations to ever take place.

Engaged in everything from business and politics to culture and social justice, young people across the globe have become a powerful force willing to overturn conventional wisdom and challenge authority. Using entrepreneurial flair and technological know-how, they have called out global leaders and regulators, disrupted industries, and attracted considerable media attention, all while reinventing culture. In other words, they think big ideas and take even bigger actions. They seem particularly adept at using capitalism to actively promote a higher social consciousness and impact.

For example, Kenneth Shinozuka, the 22-year-old CEO of SafeWander, started a company that sells a wearable device he invented seven years ago to help family members monitor the movements of elderly dementia patients.[5] And there is Shubham

Banerjee who, in 2014, founded Briago Labs, a company that makes low-cost Braille printers for the visually impaired. Banerjee, at thirteen, was the youngest entrepreneur to receive VC funding.[6]

On the pop culture front, Billie Eilish and Lil Nas X are two eclectic Gen Z artists who started their music careers on social media, quickly rose to fame, and became the superstars of the 2020 Grammy Awards. Eilish won four awards and Lil Nas X won two, marking a shift to a new generation and forging a new way of culture creation and influence. One that starts in someone's bedroom, broadcasts on social media, and then lets the public decide whether or not to join in, instead of one that is dictated by music industry executives and conventional record contracts. Both Eilish and Lil Nas X have become unofficial spokespersons of their generation, raising awareness for issues such as mental health and body positivity (Eilish) and LGBT representation (Lil Nas X).

And while every generation boasts its overachieving prodigies, what struck me most about these young people is that the traits we normally assign to older adults—wisdom, maturity, conviction, empathy, awareness, engagement, and productivity—are not the stuff of a few prodigies but rather can be found throughout an entire age demographic called Generation Z. Born between 1998 and 2016, most of them are still kids. But evidence suggests that Gen Zers, who represent roughly 25 percent of the U.S. population today, will be like nothing we've seen before. At a time when the world is mired in volatility, Gen Z is emerging, on multiple fronts, as the voice of reason and hope for our future. This is the main reason I've become so fascinated with them.

The first cohort of Gen Z came of age in 2016, a milestone that marked the beginning of a generational revolution we are about to experience in culture, work, and commerce. As they graduate from college, join the workforce, gain earning power, and vote, this 78-million-strong generation of young Americans is set to become a powerful cultural, economic, and political force. Understanding who they are, what they value, and how they think and behave will be crucial to educators, business leaders, and policy makers alike.

Yet the world may not be ready for them.

As with previous generations, we risk creating myths for the sake of simplifying what is a complex subject. It has happened before. Remember when Gen X were supposed to be "slackers"? As it turns out, members of this generation account for 51 percent of all business leadership roles around the world.[7] And then there are the Millennials, who were labeled "entitled and lazy" when they just had different values and behaviors that were hard for previous generations to grasp. In fact, the large number of Millennial entrepreneurs, executives, activists, and artists make that label hard to justify. Think Mark Zuckerberg (Facebook), David Karp (Tumblr), Michelle Phan (M beauty), Jessica Alba (The Honest Company), Andrew Mason (Groupon), and the many others who have created some of the most innovative and powerful companies of our time. Or consider activists like Malala Yousafzai, who raised awareness about women's education rights globally, and Lauren Bush, who launched FEED, a social business to fight world hunger. And there are of course bestselling Millennial artists like Beyoncé, who has broken many records during her career, including being the most-nominated woman in Grammy history.[8]

But labeling is only part of the issue. Another problem is attaching inaccurate attributes or behaviors to an entire population. For example, it became commonly accepted that Millennials were abandoning car ownership in favor of alternative, more environmentally friendly means of transportation, such as ride hailing or biking. Yet a major study by the Federal Reserve found that Millennials' views and preferences on car ownership do not differ significantly from those of previous generations.[9] Imagine a whole set of business decisions made based on this inaccurate view.

Even Gen Zers have already been subjected to these types of generalizations. In the early days of the COVID-19 pandemic when news reports emerged showing Gen Z students congregating on the beach in Florida, many were quick to label the entire generation as "irresponsible" and "selfish" and question their judgment. Yet in a study I conducted at that time, only 6 percent of Gen Z indicated that they don't follow the guidelines of social distancing and mask wearing, while the vast majority did.

These examples demonstrate the challenge any generational research faces and the need to balance between identifying broad themes that represent a generation without losing sight of the fact that there are exceptions, and that a generation is never truly homogeneous. Despite these inherent challenges, generational research is extremely valuable, as it allows us to imagine a potential future and prepare for it.

And preparation is needed—much more than you might think.

During my twenty years career as a management consultant, I saw many of my corporate clients challenged by the rise of the Millennials. They did not fit the mold of what was thought to be a "good employee." They did not follow the typical life-stage patterns that had informed marketing for years—e.g., graduate from school by a certain age, get married and buy a house by a certain age, and so on. It was confusing. Companies were not well prepared. Suboptimal decisions were made, resources were wasted, and Millennial-targeted strategies often had to be revised. It was a stormy ride.

My observations inspired me to found Gen Z Planet, a research and advisory firm that is committed to helping leaders across sectors and industries to take a more proactive approach with Generation Z. We have a one-time opportunity to get this right!

By not labeling them, by listening to what they have to say, and by embracing what they have to offer, we can avoid much of the pain that was experienced with the previous generation. Most important, we can create a path for the successful integration of Gen Z in the workforce and the consumer market and drive growth and market success. For those who are well prepared, it can be a smooth sail.

With the mission of "getting it right this time," I set out to gain deeper, fact-based insights into Gen Z. Specifically, I wanted to understand the life experiences that shaped their values and beliefs, and I wanted to know how they feel about various topics, including technology, education, career, money and consumption, social issues, and life in general. I also wanted to know them on a more personal level. What do they see as their main challenges? What are their fears, hopes, and dreams?

To answer these questions, I embarked on a journey combining primary and secondary research. My starting point was a multigenerational study of three thousand Americans, one thousand from each of three generations—Gen Zers, Millennials, and Gen Xers—which was designed to determine real points of difference between the generations. In addition, through a series of polls of smaller sample sizes, I obtained additional, mostly qualitative, insights from Gen Zers on specific issues. These studies were rounded out with a focus group with Gen Z high school girls and with in-depth interviews with twenty Gen Zers (my "Book Panel")—a wonderful group of teens and young adults from across the country who took the time to share with me how they live their lives, what is important to them, and what their plans for the future are. My research, with only a few exceptions, was focused on Gen Zers between the ages of 16 to 22 years old because this group has a certain degree of independence from their parents and relatively mature views about what they want to do as adults. This book also builds on many interviews I conducted with parents, schoolteachers, corporate executives, and founders of innovative startups who are building the companies of the future with Gen Z in mind, as well as organizational experts, psychologists, and academics.

Combining these sources and research methods with my own experience of advising global brands and retailers helped me create a 360-degree view of Generation Z and identify the implications this up-and-coming generation might have for businesses or other organizations seeking to engage them.

Finally, I felt that I cannot do justice to this generation without having a visual representation of who they are. After all, Gen Z grew up with phones in their hands, and visual communication is one of the most important factors distinguishing them from previous generations. As such, throughout my research and polls, I asked Gen Z participants to share with me their "biggest dream." In collaboration with artists from all around the world, we turned a selected number of responses into illustrations. These are shared throughout the book with the goal of providing further insight into the minds and hearts of this generation. (Note that the names and some identifying details of Gen Z participants—Book Panel and "Dreamers"— have changed to protect their privacy.)

The book is organized in three parts:

Part I examines the unique characteristics of Gen Z: who they are, the life experiences and events that have shaped their identities, values, and behaviors, and the impact that all of these will have on the ever-evolving American culture.

Part II focuses on education and career and examines the challenges that Gen Zers and their employers face as a result of the mismatch between the education they obtain and the constantly changing needs of a 21st-century workplace. In addition, this part examines the key characteristics of Gen Z as employees, their aspirations, their expectations from employers, and what is needed to effectively attract, train, retain, and integrate them into a workforce that spans multiple generations.

Part III outlines the main characteristics of Gen Z as consumers by examining their attitudes toward money, savings, and spending. It also describes Gen Z's shopping behaviors and the drivers behind them, including what these young consumers expect from brands and retailers and how to effectively market to them.

Whether you are a CEO, marketing executive, human resources executive, manager, educator, or public official, I hope reading this book will give you the necessary insights to effectively engage this remarkable generation.

MEET THE GEN Z PANEL*

Avatar illustrations by artist Selma Nached.

*All names and some identifying details have been changed to protect the privacy of the participants.

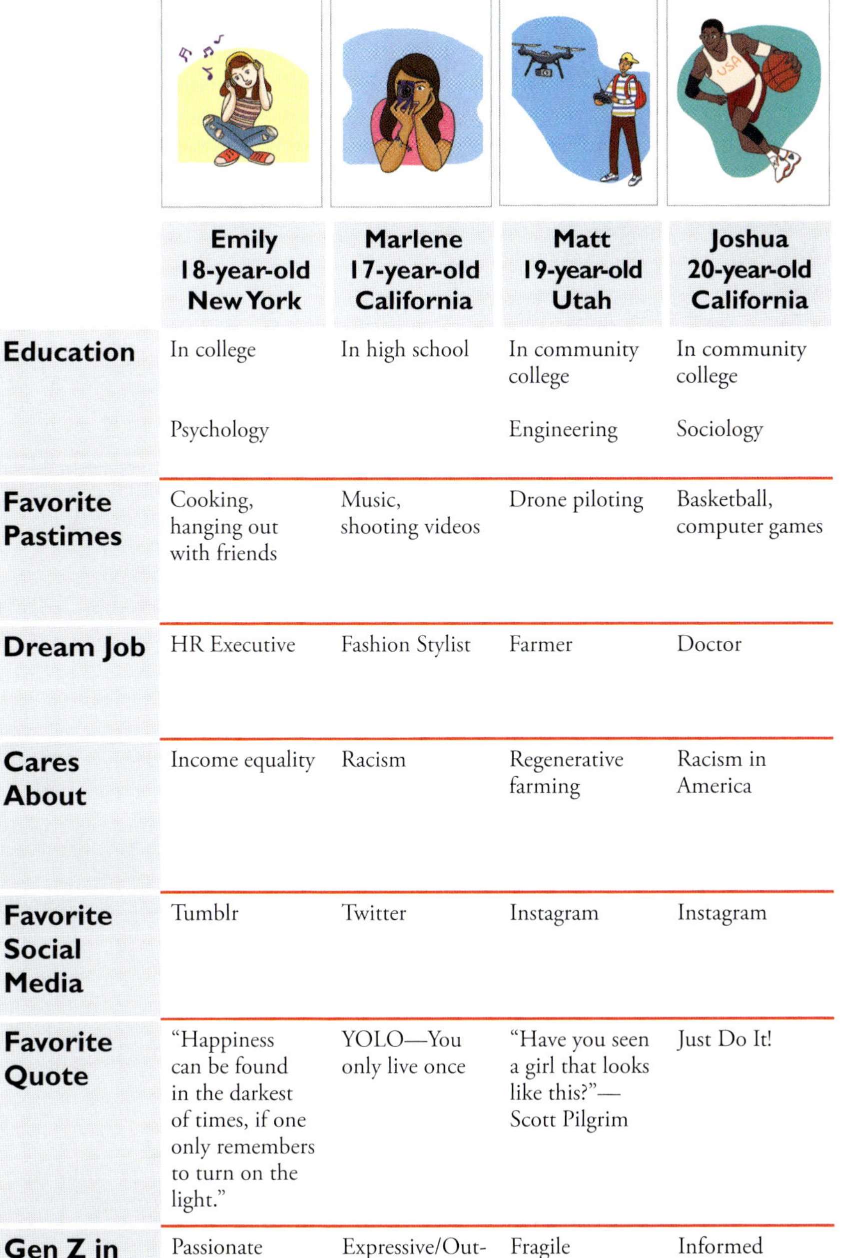

	Emily 18-year-old New York	Marlene 17-year-old California	Matt 19-year-old Utah	Joshua 20-year-old California
Education	In college Psychology	In high school	In community college Engineering	In community college Sociology
Favorite Pastimes	Cooking, hanging out with friends	Music, shooting videos	Drone piloting	Basketball, computer games
Dream Job	HR Executive	Fashion Stylist	Farmer	Doctor
Cares About	Income equality	Racism	Regenerative farming	Racism in America
Favorite Social Media	Tumblr	Twitter	Instagram	Instagram
Favorite Quote	"Happiness can be found in the darkest of times, if one only remembers to turn on the light."	YOLO—You only live once	"Have you seen a girl that looks like this?"—Scott Pilgrim	Just Do It!
Gen Z in one or two words	Passionate	Expressive/Outspoken	Fragile	Informed

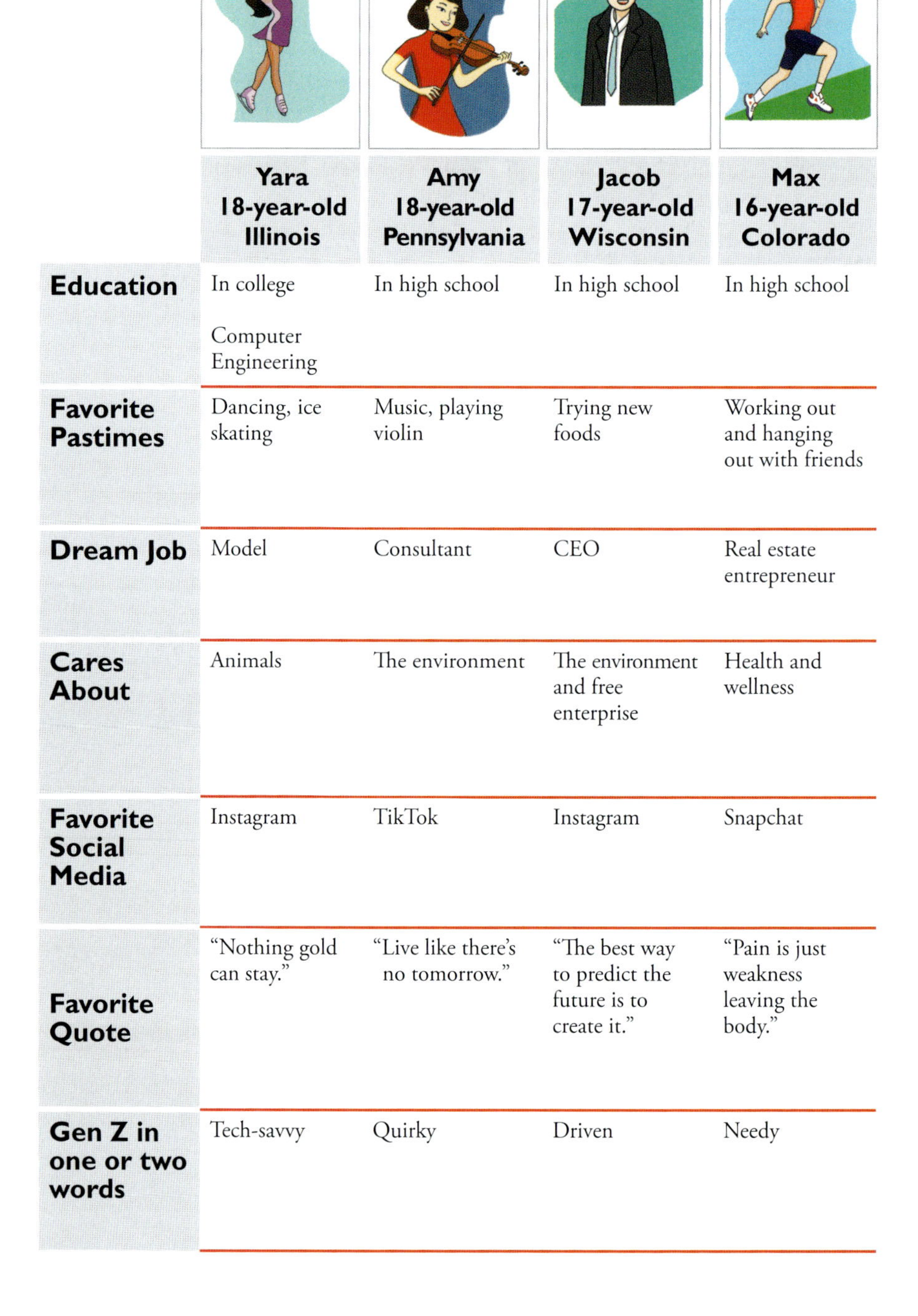

	Yara 18-year-old Illinois	Amy 18-year-old Pennsylvania	Jacob 17-year-old Wisconsin	Max 16-year-old Colorado
Education	In college Computer Engineering	In high school	In high school	In high school
Favorite Pastimes	Dancing, ice skating	Music, playing violin	Trying new foods	Working out and hanging out with friends
Dream Job	Model	Consultant	CEO	Real estate entrepreneur
Cares About	Animals	The environment	The environment and free enterprise	Health and wellness
Favorite Social Media	Instagram	TikTok	Instagram	Snapchat
Favorite Quote	"Nothing gold can stay."	"Live like there's no tomorrow."	"The best way to predict the future is to create it."	"Pain is just weakness leaving the body."
Gen Z in one or two words	Tech-savvy	Quirky	Driven	Needy

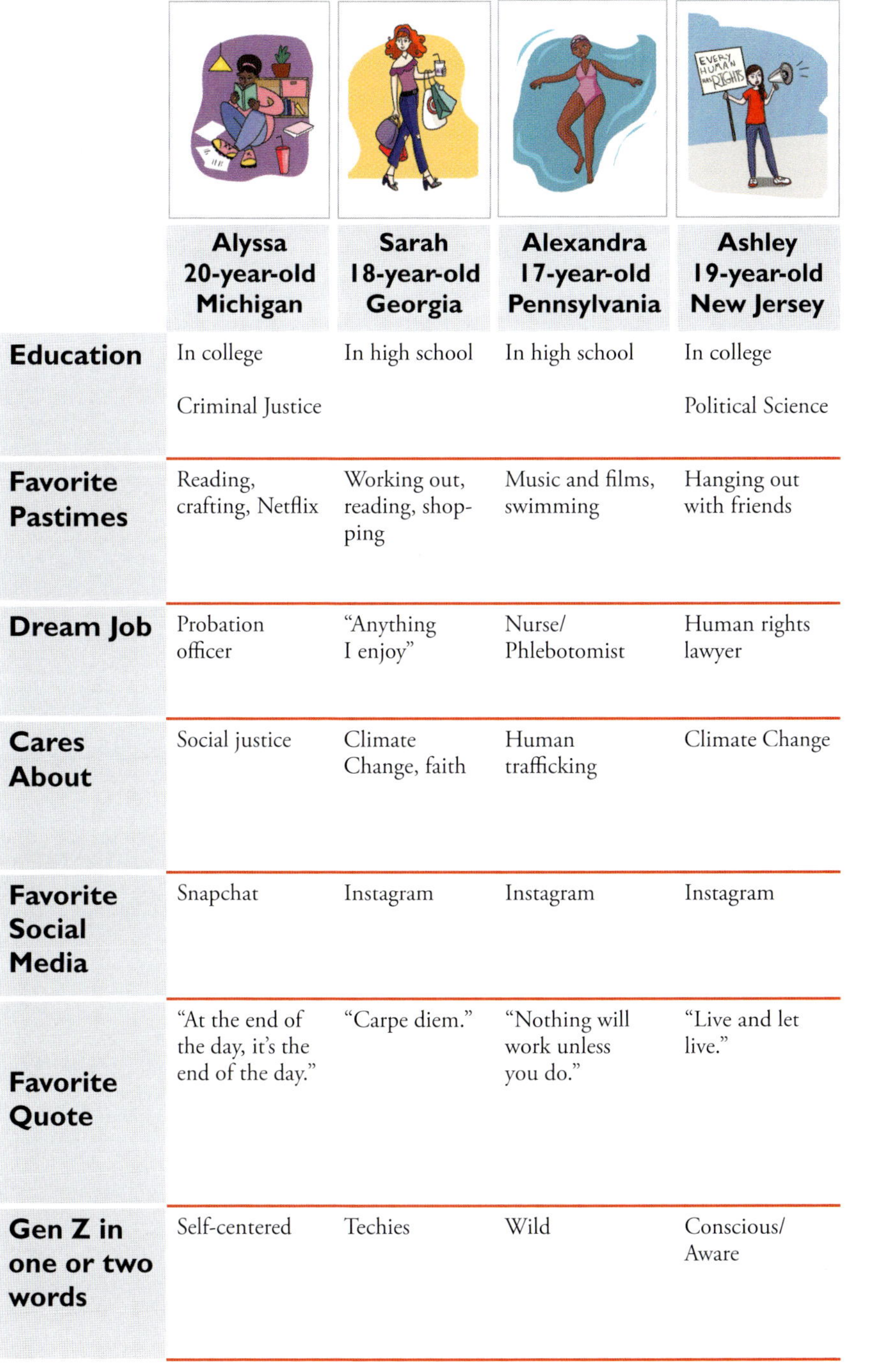

	Alyssa **20-year-old** **Michigan**	**Sarah** **18-year-old** **Georgia**	**Alexandra** **17-year-old** **Pennsylvania**	**Ashley** **19-year-old** **New Jersey**
Education	In college Criminal Justice	In high school	In high school	In college Political Science
Favorite Pastimes	Reading, crafting, Netflix	Working out, reading, shopping	Music and films, swimming	Hanging out with friends
Dream Job	Probation officer	"Anything I enjoy"	Nurse/ Phlebotomist	Human rights lawyer
Cares About	Social justice	Climate Change, faith	Human trafficking	Climate Change
Favorite Social Media	Snapchat	Instagram	Instagram	Instagram
Favorite Quote	"At the end of the day, it's the end of the day."	"Carpe diem."	"Nothing will work unless you do."	"Live and let live."
Gen Z in one or two words	Self-centered	Techies	Wild	Conscious/ Aware

	Brandon 22-year-old Virginia	**Wendy 22-year-old Maryland**	**Samantha 23-year-old Rhode Island**	**Julia 22-year-old California**
Education	College graduate Psychology	College graduate Computer Science	College graduate Fashion Merchandising & Design	College graduate Horticultural Science
Favorite Pastimes	Watching sports	Volleyball	Skiing, spending time with friends and family	Yoga, hiking, the outdoors
Current Job	Counselor, Nonprofit organization	Developer, National bank	Assistant store manager, Fashion retailer	Operations intern, Agricultural producer
Cares About	Mental health	The Environment	Effects of tech-nology on our lives	Natural treatment for mental health
Favorite Social Media	Instagram	Instagram	Not on Social Media	Snapchat
Favorite Quote	"We know what we are but know not what we may be."	"To get to the top you have to get off your bottom."	"Everything happens for a reason."	"Your energy flows where your focus goes. What you focus on grows."
Gen Z in one or two words	Compassionate	Tech addicts	Trendy	Tired of old structures

	Evan 23-year-old New York	**Taylor 17-year-old New York**	**Emma 21-year-old Arizona**	**Dylan 19-year-old Illinois**
Education	College graduate Chemical Engineering	In high school	In college Management Information Systems & Global Business	In college Software Engineering
Favorite Pastimes	Golf, Video games	Competitive rowing	Trying out new restaurants	Fixing computers, gaming
Current Job / Dream Job	Manufacturing engineer Biotech company (current)	Rowing coach	Marketing executive	Running a tech company
Cares About	World economy and health	Human rights and wealth inequality	Gender wage gap	Religion and community
Favorite Social Media	Snapchat	Instagram	TikTok	Snapchat
Favorite Quote	"We all make choices in life, but in the end our choices make us."	"Love the fight."	"Aspire to inspire."	"Don't take life too seriously, you won't come of it alive."
Gen Z in one or two words	Adaptive	Information overloaded	Creative and complicated	Learning

My dream is to stop all the suffering in the world and discover life on other planets so that we all may fly into the heavens.

Dreamer: Ryan, 19, Wisconsin
Artist: Jaen Lassalle, 36, Bordeaux, France

PART I

Culture

CHAPTER 1

Who Is Gen Z?

DEFINING THE EXACT years that form the boundaries of a generation has always been a challenge because factors such as cultural influences or the effects of landmark events can be complex and sometimes overlap across multiple generations.[10] I chose 1998 as the year that marks the beginning of Gen Z largely because it was the year that Google was founded—an event that marks the beginning of a significant acceleration in the technological breakthroughs that are going to define this generation. Perhaps it's too early to state a definite end year for Gen Z, but I'd argue that 2015 or 2016 are the potential cutoff points because the changes we have seen globally in those years, such as an increased sense of nationalism, suggests a transition of sorts between eras.

Generations, however, are defined by much more than birth years. In their book *Generations*, authors Neil Howe and William Strauss argue that a generation is "a group of people who share a time and space in history that lends them a collective persona."[11] So, to fully understand a generation, one has to take into account the full cultural, political, economic, and social context that made a lasting impact on that group during their formative years and shaped their opinions and behaviors for life (see Table 1.1). Such "cohort effects" are events that uniquely impact one generation versus another. The effects occur when people are young and impressionable and thus are most influenced by big events. For example, members of the Silent Generation, who grew up during the Great Depression in the 1930s, have said that the economic turmoil affected their attitudes toward money for the rest of their lives.

It is important to not confuse cohort effects with life-cycle effects or period effects. "When a life cycle effect is at play, differences between younger and older people are largely due to their respective positions in the life cycle."[12] As people get older, their behaviors and opinions inevitably shift depending on their life stage (think attitudes toward health care). "Period effects," however, are seen when "events and circumstances, for instance, wars, social movements, economic booms or busts, scientific or technological breakthroughs as well as broader social forces . . . simultaneously impact everyone, regardless of age."[13] As an example, think of Watergate and its impact on Americans' views of government.

This chapter provides context for the rest of the book and outlines the demographic characteristics, events, and life experiences that have shaped Gen Z's beliefs, values, and behaviors.

Table 1.1. Context Across Generations[14]

	Silent 1928-1944	Baby Boomers 1945-1964	Gen X 1965-1980	Millennials 1981-1997	Gen Z 1998-2016
Defining Events	• The Ggreat Depression • World War II	• JFK assassination • Civil Rights Movement • Vietnam War • Feminist movement • Moon landing • Watergate crisis	• Energy crisis • AIDS • 1987 stock market crash • The fall of the Berlin Wall	• Gulf War • 9/11 • War on Terror	• The Great Recession • First African American president • Hurricane Sandy • Gun violence • Black Lives Matter • #MeToo movement • COVID-19 pandemic
Family Experience	• Nuclear family • Multi-generational family	• Nuclear family • Stay-at-home moms ("the Cleavers")	• Two-income families • High divorce rate • Latchkey kids	• Helicopter parents (Boomers)	• Stealth-fighter parents (Xers) • Multi-family structures
"Game Changing" Technologies	• Car • Radio	• Integrated circuit • Color TV • Tape recorder	• Walkman • PC • Windows OS • e-mail	• Computer games • Search engines • Cell phone • E-commerce • Social media	• Smartphones • Social media • Virtual assistants • Electric cars • AR/VR • Drones
Music Stars	• Frank Sinatra • Billie Holiday • Dean Martin • Ella Fitzgerald • Louis Armstrong	• The Beatles • Bob Dylan • Aretha Franklin • Joan Baez • Carole King	• Nirvana • Guns N' Roses • Michael Jackson • Queen • Madonna	• Britney Spears • Christina Aguilera • Beyoncé • Justin Timberlake • Lady Gaga	• Ariana Grande • Drake • Zendaya • Billie Eilish • Lil Nas X
Films, Oscar Nominees/ Winners	• Citizen Kane • It's a Wonderful Life • Great Expectations • Gone With The Wind	• Love Story • A Clockwork Orange • The Godfather • Taxi Driver	• E.T. • The Breakfast Club • Star Wars • Kramer vs. Kramer	• Titanic • American Pie • The Lord of the Rings • The Matrix	• The Hate You Give • Bohemian Rhapsody • The Hunger Games • Booksmart

A Diverse Generation—In More Than One Way

In 2016, J.P. Morgan Chase aired a commercial that featured two children, a white boy and a Black girl, walking down the sidewalk holding hands. As Pat Benatar's song "We Belong" plays in the background, we see the couple age into teenagers, young adults, and finally a married couple seeking financial advice from the bank. What's remarkable about this advertisement is how utterly unremarkable it was.

Today, pop culture—everything from television and movies to advertising, comic books, and emojis—is populated with people from a diverse mix of races, sexual orientations, and genders. A gay couple is featured in a television show appropriately called *Modern Family*. The smash hit romantic comedy *Crazy Rich Asians* has an all–Asian cast. And *Hamilton,* a seminal Broadway, hip-hop–infused musical, has Black, Asian, and Latino actors playing George Washington, Thomas Jefferson, and Alexander Hamilton.

Cultural trends exert a strong influence on each particular generation. Gen Zers are growing up in a period when historically marginalized groups are gaining greater influence in society, thanks to years of activism by previous generations and to a Gen Z population that's increasingly more racially and ethnically diverse and accepting. So, a gay interracial couple plugging Cheerios cereal is not considered unusual or divisive by many younger people today, as compared to older citizens who grew up in periods that were more racially homogeneous and socially conservative.

In the summer of 2018, I had an opportunity to hold a focus group with fifteen high school girls. They traveled from all over the country to visit a leading media company in New York as part of a summer program designed to give them a glimpse into careers in media. The group consisted of Hispanics, Asians, African Americans, and whites, but none of the girls thought this mix was unusual. They had grown up in a diverse environment and knew nothing else. Certainly, every generation has witnessed the growing diversity of the population. But Gen Zers, like the high school girls, have experienced diversity at an age when they are deeply influenced by what they see and hear.

According to the U.S. Census Bureau, whites will constitute a minority of the American population by 2050,[15] a trend that is driven by factors like immigration, population growth among minorities, and interracial relationships and marriages. In 2014 America reached for the first time a point when the number of minority newborns slightly exceeded that of non-Hispanic whites[16]—"a milestone that signals the beginning of a transformation from a mostly white baby boom culture that dominated the nation during the last half of the twentieth century, to the more globalized, multiracial country that the United States is becoming."[17]

Gen Z is squarely placed in this diversity explosion, being the most diverse generation ever to live in this country. In 2019, minorities accounted for 48 percent of Generation Z. By comparison, minorities made up only 18 percent of early Baby Boomers in 1969.[18]

Demographics aside, older Gen Zers were 10 years old in 2008, when Barack Obama was elected president. They were 15 years old in 2013, when the Black Lives Matter movement began calling attention to police misconduct toward Blacks, and they were 22 years old when Darnella Frazier, a Gen Zer, captured in video the killing of George Floyd by a police officer, leading to widespread protests in which many Gen Zers participated. These events contributed to Gen Z's heightened awareness of the racial issues that America is grappling with. In my research, when asked to identify the main challenges they face as a generation, Gen Zers named racial justice among the top 10 challenges.

For Gen Z, however, diversity goes beyond race and ethnicity.

Gen Zers have witnessed a number of events that have solidified diversity in its broader sense into American consciousness: the Supreme Court decision in 2015 to legalize gay marriage, the nomination of Hillary Clinton as the Democratic Party's presidential candidate in

2016, and the #MeToo movement (2017) that brought to light issues of sexual harassment and assault against women in the workplace. As a result, Gen Zers are more aware of and are more open about issues of sexual orientation, gender identity, gender equality, and gender roles.

Based on data from my research, 76 percent of Gen Z identify as heterosexual (compared to 83 percent of Millennials and 90 percent of Gen X) while the rest of the participants identify as homosexual, bisexual, pansexual, or said they prefer not to label themselves. When I met Emily, a psychology student from Long Island, New York, we discussed sexual orientation. "I have friends who are bisexual or pansexual," she said, "and everyone is super open about it. It's not a big deal." She also pointed out that Gen Z is benefiting from the fact that society in general is more accepting than it used to be and that "people don't feel that they have to hide anymore."

Gen Zers have also become uniquely vocal about gender identity. Growing up at a time when the definitions of masculinity and femininity continue to evolve, Gen Zers are inclined to adopt a more dynamic and fluid sense of identity as a means of fully expressing themselves and questioning traditional societal constructs that they find limiting. According to Pew Research Center, 35 percent of Gen Zers say "they know someone who prefers that others use gender-neutral pronouns to refer to them," compared with a quarter of Millennials, 16 percent of Gen Xers, 12 percent of Boomers, and just 7 percent of Silents. Gen Zers are also more likely to say that "forms or online profiles that ask about a person's sex should include options other than 'man' or 'woman.' Roughly six-in-ten Gen Zers (59 percent) hold this view."[19]

In addition, throughout my interviews and discussions with Gen Zers, I repeatedly heard the phrase "I don't want to be placed in a box" when it comes to society's expectations for gender behaviors and life choices. Gen Z girls, who absorbed previous generations' messages like #girlboss and #ceilingbreaker, have their sights on fields of study, professions, and roles that are typically dominated by men. For example, the share of women enrolled in STEM fields in four-year colleges, although still low, has reached 44 percent in 2018 (up from 40 percent in 2010).[20] Many of the young women I spoke to are acutely aware that there is still a long way to go before full gender equality in the workplace or the boardrooms of corporate America is achieved, and they are ready to continue to demand and advocate for that change as they join the workforce.

Reflecting an ongoing shift in gender roles, over half of the male participants said that "stay-at-home dad" is as acceptable as "stay-at-home mom," and if consumer goods sales are any indication of changing gender norms, men's grooming has been one of the fastest-growing categories in the beauty industry in the past few years.

In summary, diversity is a central concept when thinking about Gen Z. Their demographic makeup and their exposure to race and gender issues made diversity a core value for them. They regard acceptance and tolerance as a way of life and inclusivity as non-negotiable. Seventy percent of my research participants agreed that the word "tolerance" accurately describes their generation, or as one of them said, "People should be *accepting* each other and should feel safe to be who they are." As we will see later, they bring that expectation to the workplace and to their relationships with brands.

Family Is Everything—And Families Are Changing

In the last episode of the classic TV sitcom *Leave It to Beaver*, June, the mother of Beaver and Wally, finds a box that she has not seen for a long time. In the box, among various items, is a scrapbook of old photographs, and June thinks it would be fun for the family to sit together and look through it. As they reminisce about the incidents highlighted in the photos—"Beaver's first note from school; Beaver once believing that a married neighbor lady was in love with him; Wally's first shave; Beaver running away from home … Beaver and [his friend] Larry getting caught reading Larry's sister's diary … and Wally's disastrous run for class president"[21]—they give us a window into an idyllic picture of a happy family.

For readers unfamiliar with good old sitcoms, the Cleavers epitomized the nuclear family and life in the American suburbs during the 1950s and '60s. It delivered a message about the importance of the family in forming values and providing stability and love against a backdrop of the "dangerous world out there." While many of the values the Cleavers tried to teach us are still valid, there is no doubt that the idealized "one size fits all" family structure—two parents, two kids, and a single income—is neither the most common structure nor ideal for everyone these days.

The notion of what constitutes an "American family" continues to evolve, being shaped by cultural, social, and economic forces. But whatever it is, one's family and childhood experiences still play a central role in influencing one's psyche and shaping one's values as an adult. So to understand Gen Z, we must examine their families.

Gen Zers grew up in a society where different family structures exist and, perhaps more important, are often accepted. Four types of family structures have become more common: single-parent households, multigenerational households, blended families, and same-sex couples.

One of the most striking statistics about family structures in America is the increasing number of children who are living in a single-parent household. According to the U.S. Census Bureau and the Pew Research Center, 69 percent of those under the age of 18 lived in a household with two parents in 2018,[22] compared to 87 percent in 1960.[23] In that same year, 20 million kids lived in single-parent households, and 80 percent of this group lived with a single mother. Another three million kids lived in households with no parents and were typically being raised by grandparents or other relatives.[24]

Marlene, a 17-year-old from California who was raised by her immigrant single mother, shared with me how her experience shaped her: "My mom was extraordinarily strong, and she always supported us. Seeing that she works so hard just to provide for us was inspiring to me and it makes me work harder. She showed me that I can do so much, and it makes me want to strive to do better … get an education and be financially independent."

Family structure significantly affects the economic conditions that these kids are raised in. Data shows that families with a single parent earned much less income than other family types. In 2018, 30 percent of children with a single parent lived in a household with an annual income of less than $20,000.[25] Depending on the number of household members, that income put a portion of those families below the federal poverty line. In some cases, children in these households start taking jobs while in school to help their single parents or siblings to cope with their financial responsibilities.

Joshua (20), a community college student who lives in California and plans to go to medical school, started at an early age to take on jobs and share in the household responsibilities to help his single mother. He told me, "My mom is my hero, I will do everything for her." For Matt (19), who lives in Utah, having to work while in college has placed extra pressure on him. Still, he said, "I need to help my mom pay the bills."

The second type of family structure that has become more common in past years is the multigenerational family, consisting of grandparents, parents, and children. A major factor that drives the increase is immigration. Both Latin American and Asian immigrants are more likely to live in multigenerational households. Other key factors include the increase in single parenthood; the rise in the aging population, which requires families to care for their elderly members; and economic necessity.

I wish my mom wouldn't have to work so hard.

Dreamer: David, 16, Virginia

Artist: Jone Leal, 36, Estado Zulia, Venezuela

According to Natasha Pilkauskas and Christina Cross of the University of Michigan's Gerald R. Ford School of Public Policy, the number of U.S. children living in multigenerational families increased from 5.7 percent (about 4 million) in 1996 to 9.8 percent (about 7 million) in 2016.[26]

The third type of family structure that has become more common is the blended family. This structure consists of a couple and their children from current and previous relationships. That has come about as divorce and remarriage have become more common. Sixteen percent of U.S. children are living in this type of household.[27]

Finally, a category for which traditionally there was not much data: the same-sex household. With the legalization of gay marriage and the increased prevalence of gay couples having children, we are learning more about them. According to the U.S. Census Bureau, there were just over one million same-sex households in 2019.[28] An estimated 16 percent of same-sex couples are raising children.[29]

In some ways, these family structures are just another dimension of diversity that Gen Z experienced in childhood. Meeting kids from different family backgrounds is as natural to them as other aspects of diversity.

Despite their exposure to diverse types of families, Gen Zers have one thing in common: their Gen X parents, whom historian Neil Howe has characterized as "stealth-fighter parents." Gen X parents resemble the Baby Boomer "helicopter parents," in that they actively insert themselves into their children's lives. Gen X parents just do it more quietly. "Stealth-fighter parents do not hover," Howe has said. "They choose when and where they will attack. When these Gen-X 'security moms' and 'committed dads' are fully roused, they can be even more attached, protective and interventionist than Boomers ever were."[30]

Gen Xers tend to prioritize family, open communication, responsibility, and pragmatism—values that can be clearly seen in their Gen Z kids. Gen X parents heavily involve themselves with their children's choices: how they perform in school, which activities they participate in, and whom they hang out with. They encourage their kids to be active, go the extra mile, and build that "perfect résumé," which they view as an entry ticket to a good college and a better life.

Research suggests a connection between parents' reaction to economic conditions and how closely they oversee their children and what values they try to instill in them. In a recently published book, *Love, Money, & Parenting,* Matthias Doepke and Fabrizio Zilibotti argue that a parenting style is not an accident but a behavior that can be explained by economics. "Most parents, at any time and at any place, have the same objective, namely, for their kids to be happy and do well in life given the economic conditions in play," the authors write.[31] Yet in countries like Sweden, Finland, and Germany, parents have a much more relaxed style of parenting than those in the United States, the wealthiest nation in the world. Why?

The authors point to two major trends that have emerged in the United States since the 1980s: return on education and income inequality. "Return on education" refers to the growing value of academic credentials in the U.S. job market. The median income of a college graduate is approximately 65 percent higher than that of a high school graduate,[32] and wages have become increasingly linked to the prestige of universities and the type of degrees. Throughout their research, the authors discovered that in countries with high inequality and a high return on education (which the United States is), parents are "increasingly more worried that their children will be left behind hence they push them from a tender age to achieve and succeed."[33] Remember, Gen X parents not only grew up in the 1980s, when these trends first appeared, but also suffered the greatest impact of the Great Recession after 2008. They are actively trying to ensure their children's academic and thus future financial success, and their efforts often put their children under enormous pressure.

At the same time, many Gen Xers have developed friendly and

supportive relationships with their children. Yara, an 18-year-old from Illinois, told me, "My mom is my best friend. I love my mom so much I can't imagine life without her when I go to college," a sentiment I encountered often during my interviews with Gen Zers.

Being raised by Gen X and having experienced different family types, Gen Zers have developed a great appreciation for their families, their extended communities, and the support they derive from both. When asked to rank what they value most in life, 60 percent of Gen Zers I polled listed family as their top choice, followed by financial security and friends. In addition, their appreciation for family is evident in their aspiration to form their own families at one point in the future. Seventy four percent of my research participants said they would like to be in a stable relationship or get married, and 66 percent said they would like to have children.

It's the Economy....

In his book *Children of the Great Depression*, author Russell Freedman uses pictures taken by a band of federal photographers who captured a nation in crisis in the 1930s. "The powerful black-and-white photographs of urban youth, child farm laborers, and boxcar kids convey in human terms the meaning of the economic statistics of a time when more than half of the nation's children were growing up in families that did not have enough money to provide adequate food, shelter, clothing, or medical care."[34] The photos capture not just the desperation of the economic situation but also the hope seen in the children's smiles during rare light-hearted moments, perhaps indicating the kinds of adults these kids would become. We refer to them now as the Silent Generation: determined, resilient, disciplined, patriotic, frugal, and upholding of family values. Many of these characteristics were rooted in their childhood experiences.

Eighty years on, in 2008, children did not live in conditions nearly as devastating as those of the Great Depression, but the recession still made an important mark on their lives. Events like these always do. The early members of Generation Z were between six and ten years old when the housing market bubble burst, leading to the worst economic downturn in U.S. history since the Great Depression. Loss of a job or a home in the aftermath of the financial crisis created a backdrop of anxiety and uncertainty for many Gen Zers and their families.

Amy, who moved to the United States from China just two years before the crisis, recalls her family staying at a friend's house for a few weeks and then staying in a room in a shared house before moving to a mobile home. "The first few years were very rough," she said. "We were unable to find stability, and my father was changing jobs a lot. My parents were very good [at] hiding the details from us. I did not know the financial hardship we went through until later in life. They wanted to protect me from that stress."

Researchers have been examining for years how economic hardship affects youth development. While many studies have focused on how recessions have negatively affected youth (there is often an increase in drug use and delinquency), a 2011 paper published in the *Journal of Research on Adolescence* points to more positive outcomes. The study linked economic strain during a recession with parental depression, which resulted in a diminished bond between parents and children. To compensate for this lack of connection, these children developed positive social behaviors, including making friends, showing empathy, sharing, helping others, and volunteering, all important markers for healthy relationships and personal well-being[35] and in line with the Gen Z characteristics I observed in my research.

In addition to these positive social attributes, the recession has shaped Gen Z's attitude toward money, their sense of responsibility and work ethic, and a deep need to secure their financial future. Jacob, a 17-year-old who grew up in a well-to-do suburb of Wisconsin, summed it up well:

> I have friends whose parents lost their jobs, or neighbors who lost their homes and had to move out of state or experience homelessness for a period of time. These are people with degrees that otherwise had very stable lives, but some-

> thing unpredictable like the financial market crash turned their lives around for the worse. I think that I, and others in my generation are more cautious when it comes to spending, but even more, we understand the importance of work and the importance of saving money. We are more financially literate than other generations. We see hard work and education as ways for us to create a future that has some stability.

Gen Zers' focus on financial security has also been influenced by the country's economic inequality, which continues to widen. According to the Pew Research Center, in 2018 households in the top fifth of earners brought in 52 percent of all U.S. income, more than the lower four-fifths of earners combined.[36] In 1998, the year in which the oldest Gen Zers were born, this figure stood at 49 percent.[37] As a result, they view financial security as a top priority. While still in high school or college, many of them are taking part-time jobs or have side hustles to earn money, save money, and build their résumés.

"I am earning money, and so [are] most people I know," said Jacob. "We are big savers regardless of what financial background we come from. I have friends whose parents are in the top 1 percent of income, and they still look to save everywhere they can. They will go to McDonald's instead of a sit-down restaurant or watch Netflix together in someone's house instead of going out to a movie."

Matt, who has to work, told me, "I need to earn money. I have to pay rent for my mom and stuff like that, and I got a car that I bought a year ago, so I have to pay the bills on my car. Most people in my community college work. They need to."

In my research, 64 percent of college-age participants and 46 percent of high school–age participants said they do some work to earn cash, through either a part-time job or a side hustle.

"It's not always about the money," Jacob told me. "You see many of us taking part-time jobs a little bit sooner and a little bit more seriously than you otherwise see. Many kids in my high school [are] working at least 20 hours a week, and if I compare [them] to my sister, who is three years older than me, I can see a difference in how seriously people have taken these part-time jobs. It's not only about cash but also about building résumés and ensuring better job prospects once out of college."

Unfortunately, some of these hopes for better jobs after college were interrupted, at least temporarily, by the COVID-19 global pandemic. The depth and length of the impact is not clear at this point, but if the United States enters a long recession or perhaps even a depression, Generation Z will be the first generation to experience two recessions during their formative years. That will have long-lasting effects on their lives and will further shape their already conservative attitude toward money. In a poll I conducted during the pandemic, 59 percent of the participants said that they believe they will be even more financially conservative going forward.

Change Is the Only Constant

Each generation has experienced major national and world events that left their marks. Baby Boomers were influenced by the Vietnam War and Watergate. Gen Xers lived through the AIDS epidemic and the fall of the Berlin Wall in the 1980s. Millennials suffered the September 11, 2001 terror attacks. For Gen Z, however, there was not *one* major event that left their mark but rather a *series* of events that have happened during their formative years, resulting in a deep sense that "change is the only constant" and that "everything is temporary" (see Table 1.2).

From the British Petroleum oil spill and Black Lives Matter to the Sandy Hook shootings and the European refugee crisis, Gen Zers have absorbed major events in a visceral, instantaneous way that no other generation has previously experienced—through their smartphones and social media channels. These events have informed their beliefs, attitudes, and behaviors in three major ways.

First, events like school shootings have created a sense of anxiety and instability. According to the American Psychological Association,

75 percent of Gen Z reported that mass shootings are a significant source of stress.[38] Yara described how it makes her feel: "We grew up with school shootings. . . . I always have this fear that something will happen. . . . Other generations grew up in war, doing bombing drills, but we do the 'code red drills': ... we turn the lights off, lock the window seals and doors, and hide in a corner of the room. . . . The older we got, the scarier it became because we understood what it meant."

Table 1.2. Change Is the Only Constant

Event	Year	Oldest Gen Z Age
Great Recession	2008	10
Barack Obama elected president	2008	10
Haiti earthquake	2010	12
Occupy Movement	2011	13
BP oil spill	2012	14
Sandy Hook shooting	2012	14
Hurricane Sandy	2012	14
Snowden leaks NSA data	2013	15
Black Lives Matter movement	2013	15
Ferguson uprisings	2015	17
European refugee crisis	2015	17
Supreme Court legalizes gay marriage	2015	17
Hillary Clinton is Democratic Party nominee	2016	18
Donald Trump elected president	2016	18
UK Brexit referendum	2016	18
#MeToo movement	2017	19
Parkland school shooting	2018	20
Widespread legalization of cannabis	2018	20
COVID-19 global pandemic	2020	22
George Floyd uprisings	2020	22

Second, Gen Z never had the privilege of not knowing. With the Internet at their fingertips, they are constantly exposed to national and international events. This continual exposure has contributed to a heightened sense of distrust in government and other traditional institutions that have failed to solve social and economic challenges that have persisted for decades. It has also motivated Gen Zers to speak up, take action, and advocate for change through civic engagement and volunteerism.

In a poll of a group of older Gen Zers (ages 18–22), I asked them to describe how the exposure to this list of events has shaped their lives. Here are two statements:

> "The exposure to each of these events has shaped who I am in countless ways. Going through these events and being able to be part of these movements have helped me not only become a better person, but to always remember that I have rights and I should always stand for what's right."

> "I think because of these events and many others, my generation has been introduced to society as a thing that is always changing, and [so we believe] that reform is possible. That people *can* and *do* change the world, and change is not something to be afraid of—nothing gets done if nothing changes."

Third, growing up amidst constant change has made members of Generation Z highly adaptable to new situations and challenges. Many of the executives and educators I interviewed for this book pointed out that Gen Zers' ability to deal with change is outstanding. They seem to just go with the flow—an ability that makes them an asset to both society and the workplace. Or as one of the poll's participants put it: "The constant change we faced has made me realize that we are in a transition point in history. Every event that takes place from this point on will in a way act as a test of how we can adapt and overcome whatever obstacle we are faced with, and hopefully from these events and challenges we will emerge victorious."

And if they needed any more events to test their ability to adapt, Gen

Zers are facing the challenges brought upon them by the COVID-19 pandemic. It has affected every aspect of their lives: graduation ceremonies made virtual, internships cancelled, social lives interrupted, and, for those who were employed, reduced hours, furloughs, or layoffs. Yet when I asked how they feel about their personal futures, 69 percent of my poll participants said they feel optimistic. Their optimism is rooted in the belief that "scientists [are] working around the clock to find a cure" and "humanity is quite resilient." They view the situation as an opportunity to learn about and change some of our societal deficiencies. "I feel like we will come out stronger and more united from this. We will hopefully learn more about the flaws in our systems and fix them," said one of the participants.

Finally, as the saying goes, what doesn't kill you makes you stronger. It looks as if Generation Z has developed certain strengths in response to their life experiences and the constant changes they have faced.

Ryan M. Niemiec, Psy.D., is the education director at the VIA Institute on Character, a nonprofit organization that is dedicated to the science of character strengths. The Institute's personality test that measures different dimensions of character was taken by thousands Gen Zers, and in an article in *Psychology Today*, Niemiec shared the insights that emerged from the data: "Gen Z, on average, is high in honesty, kindness, fairness, judgment/critical thinking, and love. . . . And, when compared to adults in the general population in the U.S., Gen Z scores slightly higher in their top three character strengths." In addition, he noted that "there had been a steady decrease in several strengths across all four generations—curiosity, love of learning, appreciation of beauty/excellence, gratitude, and forgiveness. Amazingly, Gen Z has bucked the trend! Gen Z has ceased those decreases by showing slight increases in all of these strengths, with the exception of gratitude."[39]

* * *

WITH THESE STRENGTHS and their emphasis on diversity, family, financial security, and civil engagement, many Gen Zers merge traditional values with progressive points of view. According to the Pew Research Center, Gen Z is more likely to hold liberal views on issues of race, the role of government, and climate change, regardless of their political inclination.[40] This combination of traditional and liberal, which on the surface seems contradictory, is one aspect that makes Generation Z complex and fascinating at the same time.

But what truly sets them apart from previous generations is their upbringing during a time of accelerated technological change. Since 1998, their birth year, we've seen the emergence of Google, social media (including Facebook, Twitter, Instagram, Snapchat, and TikTok), streaming music services such as Pandora and Spotify, 12 generations of iPhones, a variety of wearable devices, various electronic payment methods, and a host of dating apps including Tinder and Bumble.

This explosive expansion of the Internet, apps, and portable electronic devices has swept aside the old ways and dominates every aspect of our lives. Yet members of earlier generations need to stop and consider: what if this was the only world you knew? Growing up in a digital world has deeply influenced how the members of Gen Z learn, process information, communicate, consume media and products, form relationships, and get their voices heard. The full extent of effects that technology has on their lives is still emerging. Some of these effects have been positive, others less so. I will examine these effects in the next chapter.

Chapter 1: The 360 View

- Gen Z is a generation like no other. Born after 1998, this 78-million-strong cohort grew up amidst unique social, political, and economic circumstances that have had a profound impact on who they are, what they value, and what behaviors they display:
    - Gen Z is the most racially and ethnically diverse generation ever to live in the United States.
    - They grew up in a society with far more diverse family structures. Nearly 30 percent of this generation grew up in single-parent households.
    - Gen Zers' adoption of family values, open communication, responsibility, and pragmatism are the direct result of being raised by Gen X parents.
    - Gen Z is the first generation to experience two major economic downturns during their formative years, first the Great Recession of 2008 and later facing the economic effects of COVID-19.
- As a result of their upbringing and life experiences, Gen Z developed some strong core values, most notably family and community, equality, and financial security. In turn, these values are shaping their behaviors and their expectations of the world around them, including their future employers and brands.
- Gen Z's constant exposure to a series of national and international events have made them acutely aware of both human suffering and the deficiencies of traditional institutions, especially government. This exposure triggered their willingness to challenge authority, take action, and advocate for change. More important, living amidst constant change has made Gen Z highly adaptive to change—a trait that will become extremely valuable as they join the workforce.

My Biggest Dream . . .

I want to become someone who is not afraid of failure, embraces it as an opportunity for improvement, and inspires others to do the same.

Chloe, 18, North Carolina

Achieve financial security and stability.

Carlos, 18, California

For everyone to have an equal opportunity.

Hannah, 17, Pennsylvania

Get married and have a happy family.

Jennifer, 16, New Jersey

Make my mom proud.

Kaylee, 17, Colorado

My dream is to be financially independent, travel the world, have many adventures, meet interesting people, and make sure my parents are OK.

Dreamer: Luke ,17, Ohio

Artist: Maja Tomljanovic, 41, Samobor, Croatia

CHAPTER 2

Digital Everything: The Bad, the Ugly, and the Good

ANYONE WHO ASKS a Gen Zer, "What role does technology play in your life?" is guaranteed to receive a confused look at best and rolled eyes at worst. Technology does not play a role in their life. Technology *is* their life. The Internet to Gen Z is like water to human survival—an essential, omnipresent component of everyday life, yet a resource that people hardly ever think about (unless it's unavailable).

Gen Z was born into a digital world. They don't know a time without search engines, social media, and mobile phones. This generation has no memory of devices like rotary phones, cassette tapes, TV antennas, or paper maps. And while new technology affects all generations, older Americans have perspective. They know what life was like before the technology existed and how such technology has affected their lives since. We joke, "How could we ever find each other in a busy mall before we had a cell phone?" but Gen Zers pride themselves on having the best location app.

As the true digital natives, they were using mobile devices earlier than the previous generation. By age 15, 87 percent of Gen Zers had access to a cell phone, compared to 41 percent of Millennials at the same age. In fact, some Gen Zers had a cell phone before they were 10 years old (see Figure 2.1).

Figure 2.1. The First Cell Phone

Q: How old were you when you got your first cell phone?

Percentage of respondents

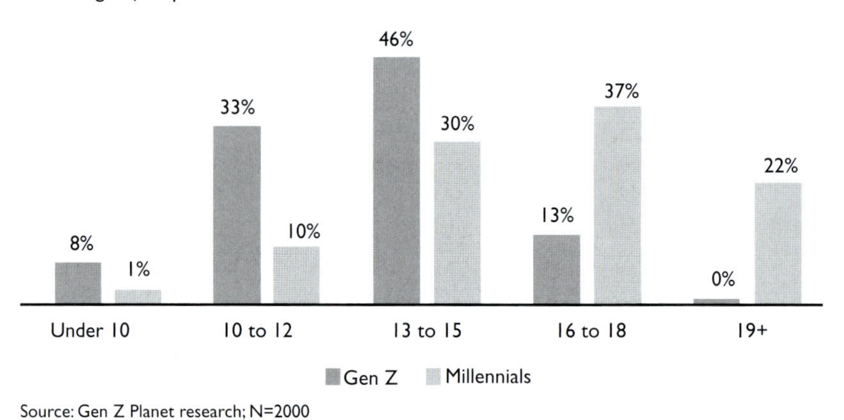

Source: Gen Z Planet research; N=2000

They also spend more time online than any other generation. Sixty-six percent of my research participants reported that they check their devices "multiple times every hour," compared to 56 percent of Millennials and 49 percent of Gen Xers.

Checking a device "multiple times every hour" translates into many hours of screen time. Common Sense Media, a nonprofit organization that helps families and schools teach kids how to navigate the digital world, published a study reporting that the average screen time for teens is in excess of seven hours a day, and for tweens it is over four hours a day—figures that do not include screen time dedicated to homework.[41] Most of that time online is spent on social media, with YouTube, Instagram, Snapchat, and TikTok being the most popular platforms. Seventy percent of my research participants listed social media as one of their top three Internet activities, followed by listening to music and watching videos (see Figure 2.2).

Figure 2.2. Gen Z Online Activity

Q: How do you spend most of your time online?
Pick your top three activities.

Percentage of Gen Z respondents

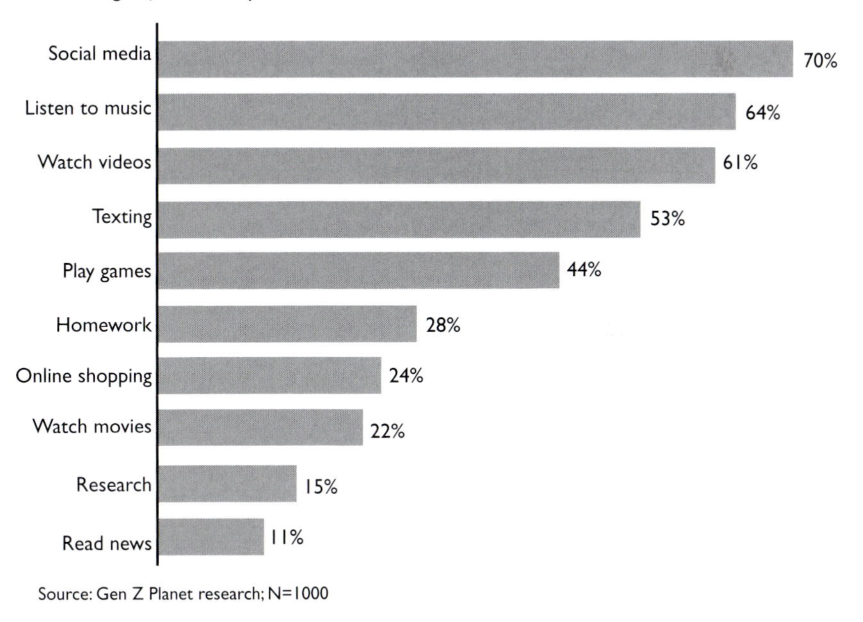

Source: Gen Z Planet research; N=1000

But Gen Zers are not just passive consumers of technology. They use it to connect, to engage, to educate themselves, and to create content of their own. It makes them pioneers of cultural creations in a way that was not possible before. Technology also offers Gen Zers a powerful platform for social activism and entrepreneurship. Thanks to social platforms, Gen Zers can create and distribute media content, start movements, create new businesses, and stay informed about international and national events.

Familiarity with technology, online information, and the means to exchange and shape it have had significant impacts on members of this generation—some bad, some ugly, and some good. While the research on these impacts is still in its infancy, understanding several emerging themes could be useful for educators, employers, and marketers as they engage with Gen Z.

The Bad

A study led by Jean Twenge, a psychology professor at San Diego State University, found that for teenagers, more screen time is correlated with less happiness. Specifically:

> Adolescents who spent more time on electronic communication and screens (e.g., social media, texting, electronic games, Internet) were less happy, [were] less satisfied with their lives, and had lower self-esteem. . . In contrast, adolescents who spent more time on non-screen activities such as in-person social interaction, sports/exercise, print media, and homework had higher psychological well-being.[42]

Some of the Gen Zers I interviewed could relate to these findings. Jacob spoke about the "unsocial side of social," saying, "Social media can make people feel bad, or make people feel that they are not part of whatever trend is going on. . . that they are not part of whatever happens socially. For example, people have a party and it was posted on social media, but those who were not invited feel left out."

Amy described the immense pressure she felt watching her peers post on social media: "I am seeing what people are doing on social media, and they all seem so successful and happy. People are only posting the best version[s] of themselves: the best selfies, the best moments. It can have a bad impact on people, especially kids who lack the self-control and go on a social media binge for hours, which I definitely was doing.

It made me feel depressed, inadequate, and demotivated. So I had to stop being on social media for a few months."

Regardless of the type of online activity, the sheer amount of screen time alone seems to have an impact on the brain and, for children and youth, on brain development. "The truth is that today we know very little [about] the impact of screen time on the brain or behaviors," Florence Breslin, manager of clinical assessments and testing at the Laureate Institute for Brain Research in Oklahoma, told me. "In fact, society is in an ongoing experiment considering how new the technology is and how rapidly it is changing."

Breslin works as an investigator on the Adolescent Brain Cognitive Development Study (ABCD), the largest longitudinal study of brain development and child health ever conducted in the United States. Her team is investigating, among other things, the relationship between screen time and brain development. Early findings from the ABCD Study indicate a correlation between screen time and an early maturation of the brain. Kids who have spent more than four hours a day on screens, on average, exhibit premature thinning of the cerebral cortex, compared to kids who have spent less time on screens. The prefrontal cortex is the area of the brain responsible for "executive functioning"—that is, complex cognitive functions like planning, problem solving, decision making, and moderating social behavior.

It is important to note that at this point researchers can only point to a correlation. They have not established a causal relationship between screen time and brain structure, nor have they determined the implications of these findings. Nevertheless, their interviews and data show that kids who spent more than four hours a day using screens got lower scores on thinking and language tests. In other words, screen time was correlated with lower "crystalized intelligence"—a term for those abilities that are more dependent on experience, as they represent accumulated stores of verbal knowledge or skills, and rely more heavily on education and cultural exposure.

Yet this is not a simple story. According to Breslin, "Some kids are doing fine with more extensive screen time and some aren't. One big differentiator is the type of content being consumed. *Content is not created equal.* Kids using social media, texting or "FaceTiming" with their friends report less sleep problems than those who spend most of their time playing video games. . .Those playing video games showed higher crystalized intelligence scores [because of the experiential nature of gaming]."

While the ABCD Study and other ongoing research are still far from any clear-cut conclusions, they all indicate that kids and youth today are processing information, learning, and playing in different ways than older generations, and that educators and employers need to take these into account when thinking about curriculum building or skill development.

The Ugly

With teens so connected online, cyberbullying has become a major problem. According to the Pew Research Center, 59 percent of U.S. teens have been bullied or harassed online. Common types of harassment include being called names, having false rumors spread about them, receiving unwanted texts or images (often explicit), being constantly asked where they are and what they're doing, and having their photos shared without their consent.[43]

"If your account is public and all sorts of random people can view or comment on your posts, you open the door to some unwanted stuff and mean messages," Marlene told me. "I have friends who got inappropriate photos on direct messaging; guys send pictures of themselves naked or ask the girls to share 'nudz' pics. It really impacted them negatively. . . . They felt objectified and ashamed."

The effects of bullying can get even worse. Stories about teens committing suicide after being bullied have made multiple headlines in recent years. Channing Smith, a 16-year-old from Tennessee, took his own life after two classmates outed him as bisexual on social media,[44] and Rosalie Avila, 13, from California, hanged herself after being bullied at school and on social media by classmates who insulted her and called her ugly.[45] These are only a few examples of the less appealing side of the digital world. And while the Centers for Disease Control suggests that "the relationship between bullying and suicide is complex" and that "most young people who die by suicide have multiple risk factors; and most young people who are bullied do not become suicidal," it does acknowledge the research that indicates that "persistent bullying can lead to or worsen feelings of isolation, rejection, exclusion, and despair, as well as depression and anxiety, which can contribute to suicidal behavior."[46]

Schools and youth employers have a lot at stake and a major role to play in reducing cyberbullying. Offering ongoing education to youth, introducing "no tolerance" policies, and providing support to those in need, are just few actions organizations can take to curb bullying, as well as educating adults on the signs to watch for to prevent suicide.

Another less appealing side of the digital life is teen participation in activities that could be harmful. For example, consider the injuries that occurred as a result of attempts to take selfies in locations that could pose danger like waterfalls or high cliffs, or the recent TikTok "Benadryl Challenge" that encouraged users to overdose on the over-the-counter drug to induce hallucination, a "challenge" that ended up with a few teens dead. "Living for the [social media] post" is certainly something that some Gen Zers have taken to an extreme.

Finally, there's digital addiction. Another report by Common Sense Media found that "50 percent of teens 'feel addicted' to mobile devices, and 59 percent of their parents agree that their kids are addicted." Most Gen Zers I interviewed admitted that they keep their phones by their bed at night, that they *often* check their phones as soon as they wake up, and that they feel the need to react immediately to posts or texts they receive. FOMO is real!

Critics say addiction is not an accident. It is a result of how the technology was designed.

Tristan Harris, a former Google product manager, is the director and a co-founder of the Center for Humane Technology, an organization that seeks to realign technology with humanity.[47] In an interview with *60 Minutes*, Harris described the cell phone as a slot machine. "Every time I check my phone, I'm playing the slot machine to see, what did I get? This is one way to hijack people's minds and create a habit to form a habit. . . . What you do is you make it so when someone pulls a lever, sometimes they get a reward, an exciting reward. And it turns out that this design technique can be embedded inside of all these products."[48] The reward that Harris is talking about is the chance of receiving "likes," followers, emojis, or text messages. Such a system leaves users in a constant state of anxiety, hobbled by a constant desire to check their devices.

He also believes that parents do not fully understand the impact on their children. "There's a narrative that, oh, I guess they're just doing this like we used to gossip on the phone. But what this misses is that your telephone in the 1970s didn't have a thousand engineers on the other side of the telephone who were redesigning it to work with other telephones and then updating the way your telephone worked every day to be more and more persuasive. That was not true in the 1970s."

In recent years, however, Gen Zers (and their parents and teachers) are increasingly exposed to concepts such as digital citizenship—a term that refers to the responsible use of technology. Programs, like those offered by Common Sense Media or the International Society for Technology in Education, have emerged to address some of the negative aspects of technology use by youth. These and similar programs address media balance, e-mail etiquette, online bullying, and online safety, as well as misinformation, distinguishing fact from fiction, using technology to engage in civic action, and allowing for different opinions and points of views to be heard.

The Good

On the flip side, plenty of research suggests that technology usage produces strong benefits for young people. Dr. Andrew Przybylski, an experimental psychologist at Oxford University, and Dr. Netta Weinstein of Cardiff University co-authored a paper arguing that "moderate use of digital technology is not intrinsically harmful and may be advantageous in a connected world. . . . This may be because digital connectivity can enhance creativity, communication skills and development."[49]

"We are very artistic," said Marlene. "A lot of us are getting into writing music, photography and video making and editing. I do blogs. . . . I am in a program at school where we do video editing. We go out, shoot art and then edit."

Platforms such as Pinterest, Tumblr, TikTok, and Instagram allow everyone to be a photographer, designer, or curator of "moments" and "favorite things" and to showcase their creativity. Seventy-four percent of my research participants agreed that social media allows them to be more creative, and 81 percent viewed it as a vehicle for self expression (see Figure 2.3).

Figure 2.3. The Positive Effects of Social Media

Q: To what extent do you agree or disagree with the statement?

Percentage of Gen Z who answered "agree" or strongly agree"

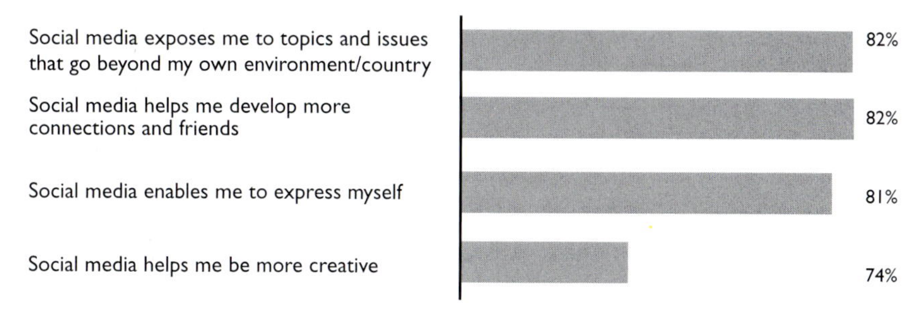

Source: Gen Z Planet research: N=1000

Social media also allows Gen Zers to stay informed about international and national events. I asked my research participants to share how they feel about a list of statements describing the impact of social media. The vast majority (over 80 percent) agreed that social media exposes them to topics and issues that are beyond their own immediate concerns and their own country, contributing to a greater level of understanding and empathy they feel toward others, than they would have otherwise. "Through social media, I'm exposed to issues I would have no way of knowing existed in the first place," wrote one participant. Others pointed to the "realness" and visceral nature of some of the stories they encounter, stories that are often told by "real people" who used their cell phones to document events, sometimes historical, in their own authentic voice. From the protests in Hong Kong to the devastating effects of COVID-19 on young people in developing countries, Gen Zers are more aware and as a result more inclined to take action. "We are the most informed generation," Joshua told me, "and being informed, makes you think, makes you want to take action and strive to bring positive change."

In addition, 82 percent of my research participants view the ability to form new connections, make new friends locally and globally, and keep in touch, as positive aspects of social media. As Jacob summed up: "There is the overall connection we have with one another. I have friends who moved away, but I am still part of their lives in some weird way in this digital universe. Our social lives are really facilitated by social media."

Finally, in a post-coronavirus world, Gen Z, thanks to their digital savviness, may be uniquely positioned for a new era of interactions where education, commerce, and work will partially shift online. Gen Zers will adapt faster and potentially can help others to adapt, too.

What emerges from all of the trends that have developed during the rise of this generation is the pervasive nature of tech in Gen Zers' choices. Whether online activity leads to loneliness or bullying or wider connections, that is the world they are growing up in and that is the way they experience it. Yet their radical new environment is not producing an entirely radical new generation. In fact, in some aspects of their lives Gen Zers are emerging as somewhat more traditional.

Chapter 2: The 360 View

- Gen Z was born into a digital world. They don't know a time without search engines, social media, and cell phones. The vast majority of this generation had access to a cell phone by the time they were 15 years old and they spend more time online than any other generation (at least 7 hours a day, by one count). Most of this time is spent on social media, listening to music, and watching videos.
- The research of the long-term effects of screen time on youth is still in its infancy, but early findings point to a correlation between long screen time and early maturation of the brain as well as lower overall well-being. One thing is clear, however, kids and youth today are processing information, learning, and playing in different ways than older generations. Educators and employers need to take these into account when thinking about curriculum building and skill development.
- Cyberbullying, participation in harmful digital challenges, and digital addiction are the some of the less appealing consequences of living in a digital world. These negative aspects place additional pressure on schools and youth employers to develop solutions that address these issues and provide support to those in need.
- The digital world, however, is not only bad and ugly. Gen Zers use technology to connect, to engage, to educate themselves, and to create content of their own. It makes them pioneers of cultural creations in a way that was not possible before. Technology also offers Gen Zers a powerful platform for social activism and entrepreneurship.
- In a post-coronavirus environment, Gen Z, thanks to their digital savviness, may be uniquely positioned for a new era of interactions where education, commerce, and work will partially shift online. Gen Zers will adapt faster and may be able to help others to adapt, too.

I wish I was thin.

Dreamer: Sofia, 20, Arizona

Artist: Jasmijn Evans, 28, Zwolle, The Netherlands

CHAPTER 3

The End of Youth as We Know It

NO FILM CAPTURED the idea of teenage rebellion like *The Breakfast Club*. It depicted a day in the life of five stereotypical teenagers in school detention: Bender, the criminal, who pulled a fire alarm; Claire, the princess, who skipped school to go shopping; Andrew, the jock, who humiliated a nerdy classmate; Brian, the brain, whose flare gun accidently went off in his locker; and Allison, the basket case, who had nothing better to do but attend detention. The students pass the hours by talking about school, family, and sex and smoking marijuana. They openly defy the authority of an arrogant, overbearing teacher assigned to oversee their detention, and they share their personal challenges and angst.

Society has long associated youth with being rebellious, self-centered, and carefree, but Gen Z is changing this "formula." While teenagers have historically engaged in risky behaviors like sex, drinking, and drug use, Gen Zers have remained relatively mild. Having absorbed the experiences of previous generations, Gen Zers have demonstrated behaviors that completely upend the typical narrative of youthful rebellion.

"Teens aren't what they used to be," Professor Jean Twenge of San Diego State University wrote in an article. "The teen pregnancy rate has reached an all-time low. Fewer teens are drinking alcohol, having sex or working part-time jobs. Teens are also now less likely to drive, date or go out without their parents than their counterparts 10 or 20 years ago."[50]

But Gen Z is far from being carefree.

In my research, when asked to describe the key challenges of their generation, Gen Zers provided a long list, including pressure to succeed, obesity and body image issues, financial insecurity, political conflict, societal divisions, race and economic inequality, and gun violence. These challenges contribute to one of the most prominent challenges they described—mental health.

Reversing the Trend

We have long equated adolescence with rebellion, and with good reason. Teens are transitioning from childhood into adulthood. They are separating from their parents, forming identities, and seeking to make independent decisions. But in recent decades that rebellion has defied common expectations—the very essence of rebellion!

Since 1991, the Centers for Disease Control has been publishing the Youth Risk Behavior Surveillance (YRBS), which surveys more than 10,000 high school students every couple of years about activities ranging from use of alcohol and drugs to smoking, sexual behavior, and violence.[51] The federal data show that the percentage of teens who say they engage in such behaviors has dropped significantly over the past few decades (see Table 3.1), a trend that has continued to decline, sometimes sharply, since 2013, the year the YRBS started to measure Gen Zers. For example, 29 percent of high school kids reported trying cigarettes in 2017 compared to 41 percent in 2013; although the increase in vaping accounts for some of that drop, this is still a significant drop. Similarly, the percentage of kids who have consumed alcohol dropped to 60 percent in 2017 from 66 percent in 2013.

Table 3.1. Youth Risky Behavior, 1991–2019 (Selected Indicators)

	1991	2001	2011	2013*	2015	2017	2019
Unintentional injury and violence							
Rarely or never wore a seat belt	26%	14%	8%	8%	6%	6%	6%
Carried a weapon (gun, knife)	26%	17%	17%	18%	16%	16%	13%
Tobacco use							
Ever tried a cigarette	70%	64%	45%	41%	32%	29%	24%
Currently smoke cigarettes	27%	28%	18%	16%	11%	9%	6%
Currently use electronic vapor products at least once in the past 30 days					24%	13%	32%
Alcohol and drugs							
Ever tried alcohol	82%	78%	71%	66%	63%	60%	n/a
Currently drink alcohol	51%	47%	39%	35%	33%	30%	29%
Ever used marijuana	31%	42%	40%	41%	39%	36%	36%
Ever used cocaine	6%	9%	7%	6%	5%	5%	4%
Sexual behavior							
Ever had sexual intercourse	54%	46%	47%	47%	41%	40%	38%
Had sexual intercourse before the age of 13	10%	7%	6%	6%	4%	3%	3%

* 2013 is Gen Z's first year in high school.

Source: Centers for Disease Control, 1991–2019, high school youth risk behavior survey data

So what's driving these numbers?

The first factor is parenting. Gen X parents, as we have seen earlier, are very protective; they spend more time monitoring what their kids do and give more explicit guidance. Another factor is technology; because kids spend more time at home with their smartphones and less time socializing in person, they have fewer opportunities to engage in risky behaviors. Finally, kids have been repeatedly exposed to programs and public service campaigns designed to curb some of these behaviors. "It's true that we are a little more risk-averse when it comes to things like drinking or drugs, or being more sexually active," said Jacob. "It's the upbringing we had. There was a hard effort against drugs and alcohol and drinking and driving. I remember seeing movies as a kid, and part of the trailer was an advertisement against drugs and alcohol."

Teen pregnancy is another indicator. It has been on the decline for decades, but Gen Z has further accelerated the decline. In 2018, the birth rate for females aged 15–19 was 17.4 births per 1,000 women, a figure that represents a 52 percent decline since 2013, compared to a 41% decline in the previous five years.[52]

This trend is also influenced by various factors, including educational programs, media, close parenting, and learning from others. Marlene told me that her aunt got pregnant at an early age and couldn't finish high school. "I feel that it was one of her biggest life regrets," she said. "Frankly, many of us have seen the consequences of teen pregnancy and have taken precautions so we won't end up with these kinds of regrets. . . . I feel that as a generation, we learned from other people's mistakes. Though teens still drink and do drugs, it is not wild because we were told by our parents so many times not to do it and it just sank in."

Media has also played a role. For example, the MTV show *16 and Pregnant,* which ran from 2009 to 2014 before being renewed in 2020, followed the lives of teenagers during the final months of their pregnancies and early months of motherhood. Illustrating how difficult it is to have a child at a young age, the show highlighted the strain that parenthood puts on young mothers, including sleep deprivation, challenging relationships with the father of the child, the effect on their relationships with their own family and friends, in addition to the challenge of fulfilling school commitments.

A study by the National Bureau of Economic Research that measured the impact of media on social outcomes found that this show accounted for a 4.3 percent reduction in teen pregnancy in the 18 months following its introduction. Analysis of search-engine and tweeting activity indicated that the show prompted young people to search for information and learn more about teen pregnancy, abortion, and contraception.[53]

Still, for girls who happen to give birth during their teen years, the biggest challenge is completing their education. Overall, only half of teen mothers received a high school diploma, which affects their employment prospects and future economic outcomes.[54]

Gen Z is no doubt reversing the trends long associated with teens. Some see the decline in risky behavior as indication of their lack of maturity or lack of willingness to become adults. But what if Gen Z is just more responsible?

David Finkelhor, a professor of sociology and director of the Family Research Laboratory at the University of New Hampshire, thinks exactly that. In his article "Are Kids Getting More Virtuous?" he shared this view: "By many measures, young people are actually showing virtues their elders lacked. They have brought delinquency, truancy, promiscuity, [and] alcohol abuse down to levels unseen in many cases since the 1950s. Rather than coming up with ever more old-fogey complaints, we should be celebrating young people's good judgment and self-control—and extolling their parents and teachers."[55]

Far from Carefree

"Gen Z is anxious, distrustful, and often downright miserable," said *Inc.* magazine. "Generation Z is stressed, depressed and exam-obsessed," claimed *The Economist*. "Why Are More American Teenagers Than Ever Suffering from Severe Anxiety?" asked a *New York Times* headline.

Several studies suggest that these sentiments are not mere anecdotes. Data from the CDC suggests that Gen Zers are struggling with mental health problems like depression, anxiety, and suicide. Among persons aged 10–24 the number of suicides per 100,000 people jumped from 6.8 in 2007 to 10.6 in 2017. During this period, the suicide rate for persons aged 10–14 nearly tripled.[56]

Blue Cross Blue Shield data confirms that diagnosis rate for major depression among adolescents increased by 63 percent between 2013 and 2016.[57] And according to the Center for Collegiate Mental Health, in 2018, 54 percent of college students attended counseling for mental health concerns, up from 46 percent in 2010.[58] In a survey conducted by health insurance giant Cigna, at least 60 percent of Gen Zers identified with 10 of 11 feelings associated with loneliness, including "feeling like people around them are not really with them," "feeling shy," "feeling like no one really knows them well," "feeling alone," and "feeling left out."[59]

Clearly, young people today are far from being carefree and untroubled. My research participants indicated mental health issues as a main challenge for them and their peers.

When Matt was a senior in high school, he suffered a major crisis. He needed scholarships to pay for college, but the stress and pressure to get good grades overwhelmed him. "I kind of broke under it and developed general anxiety disorder and panic disorder," he said. "It was a rough experience at first, but then I was on medications and I kept seeing a therapist, so I learned the tools that I needed to cope with things and gradually came off the medication."

What sets Gen Zers like Matt apart from previous generations is their willingness to confront the issue, thanks to exposure to outside information, either from other people or from the Internet. The fact that discussing mental illness carries less stigma in society also helps. "When I was going through it, I felt really embarrassed, especially because I feel that boys are not supposed to have issues like this," Matt said. "But then a lot of my friends started to talk to me about similar experiences."

So, what is causing the increase in mental health incidents among young people?

For one thing, society better understands mental illness as a health condition that requires treatment. Patients are more open to seeking help. "There is a great deal of openness about mental health issues, and people are more readily seeking help," said Ashley, a 19-year-old from New Jersey who is currently studying political science at a university in California. "It is awesome that therapy is now 'normal,' and that there is no stigma or the 'hush hush' mentality of the past."

Second, experts frequently cite technology, specifically social media, as a contributor to mental illness. In her book *iGen,* Jean Twenge, the San Diego State University professor, argued that "the sharp rise in depressive symptoms among college students occurred almost exactly at the same time that smartphones became ubiquitous." She attributes the depression to the various effects of technology, including lack of in-person interaction, peer pressure on physical appearances, and even to a lack of sleep as increasing numbers of adolescents and young adults stay on their screens well into the night.[60]

In my interviews, Gen Zers, especially young women, frequently mentioned pressure regarding physical appearance. They described their disenchantment with a selfie culture that puts strong pressure on looks and their distaste for bullying and body shaming that have become prevalent. Over the past few years we've witnessed a movement to counteract body shaming by promoting a view of "body positivity," but many Gen Zers find the message hard to follow.

"Body positivity is something I think is a major challenge for my generation," Ashley told me. "The majority of the girls I met in college had some eating disorder. Every single one of them is dealing with some sort of 'emotional thing' even if nothing major happened in their lives. There is also anxiety and depression in some cases that cause eating disorders, [so it is] hard to stay positive." Along the same lines, one high school girl in my focus group said, "There is a constant message of 'celebrate and accept your body' or 'you are beautiful as you are,' but that is not always an authentic message. No one can accept themselves all the time. We need a message that says it's okay not to like your body sometimes. It will be more realistic." That is a good hint for readers who market to Gen Z girls.

In addition, Gen Z's exposure to a 24/7 news cycle contributes to stress and anxiety. In its recent report on stress in America, the American Psychological Association found that "around three in five Gen Z adults and Millennials say they want to stay informed but that following the news causes them stress." This is compared to only half of Xers and Boomers who express the same sentiment.[61]

A third contributor to the increase in reported rates of mental illness is that Gen Zers feel enormous pressure to excel academically. "School for me is the greatest source of stress," Ashley said. "We feel as if someone tells us every day, 'Your future is depending on your grades,' [or] 'You need to meet GPA requirements to get a good job.' It's very competitive and we all feel that we must succeed or be left behind."

Finally, the COVID-19 pandemic may become another contributor to worsening mental health conditions for Gen Z (if not for nearly everyone). Of the Gen Zers I polled during the pandemic, 40 percent said they felt anxious or depressed following the outbreak, mostly due to abrupt changes in circumstances, social isolation, and uncertainty about their studies or job situations.

As the evidence increases for rising mental health problems among Gen Zers, the implications for the workplace and for brands are significant. Employers need to understand this challenge and prepare to support the well-being of these newcomers, especially in an environment where remote working becomes more common. Brands will have to rethink what role they can play in supporting the mental health of their customers through either products or content.

Cautious and anxious: those are the new bywords in the information age. A world at everyone's fingertips is also a world that brings all of its pressures to weigh on this generation. It is hardly any wonder, then, that Gen Z has embraced its own vibrant culture with such enthusiasm. As we'll see in the next chapter, theirs is truly a world where anyone can make a contribution.

Chapter 3: The 360 View

- Society has long associated youth with rebellion, self-centeredness, and a carefree attitude, but Gen Z is changing this "formula." According to the CDC's Youth Risky Behavior Teen Surveillance report, teen risky behaviors are in decline, a trend that is attributed to a host of factors including increased use of technology and the associated decrease in social interaction, Gen X's parenting style, national education programs, the media, and Gen Zers being truly more responsible.
- But Gen Zers are far from carefree. They are struggling with mental health problems like depression and anxiety, and suicide rates among teens and young adults are on the rise. Several factors explain the increase in mental health issues, including greater openness in society to discuss the topic and therefore willingness to ask for help, technology use and the social isolation associated with it, higher peer pressure on physical appearance, exposure to the 24/7 news cycle, pressure to excel academically, and more recently COVID-19 and its effects on Gen Z's social lives and future economic prospects.
- As the evidence for rising mental health problems among Gen Zers increases, the implications for the workplace and for brands are significant. Employers need to understand this challenge and prepare to support the well-being of these newcomers, especially in an environment where remote working becomes more common. Brands will have to rethink what role they can play in supporting the mental health of their customers through either products or content.

My dream is to be free and cured from all my severe mental health problems.

Dreamer: Victoria, 18, North Carolina

Artist: Tatiana Boiko, 30, Novosibirsk, Russia

CHAPTER 4

Culture—Redefined

IN 2018, LIL NAS X was a struggling singer-songwriter and a college dropout living on his sister's couch in Atlanta and sharing funny memes and music clips with a relatively small number of Twitter followers. Then his debut single "Old Town Road," which he independently released on the music sharing platform SoundCloud, became an overnight success, topping the Hot Country Songs chart. By 2019, the song, which fuses hip-hop with country music, had been streamed 2.5 billion times on various music platforms in the United States alone.[62] With its catchy tune and cowboy references, it landed perfectly in the welcoming arms of TikTokers, who soon created memes and short video clips with the hashtag #oldtownroad generating close to 900 million views in less than two years after the song was released.

In the process, an unexpected obstacle appeared.

In the spring of 2019, *Billboard*, monitoring the climb of the song on its country chart, kicked it off the chart, saying, "It does not embrace enough elements of today's country music to chart in its current version."[63] The decision stirred a national debate about genre definition, race, and the music industry as well as an online backlash from fans who regarded it as discrimination against someone (a Black, gay rapper who also performs country music) who doesn't easily fit in Nashville's mostly white artist community. But the controversy also sparked an unlikely collaboration. Country legend Billy Ray Cyrus, who became aware of the situation and saw the potential in Lil Nas X, stepped in to offer support. The two recorded a new version of the song, and it ended up on the Billboard Hot 100 songs for nineteen weeks, breaking all previous records for the chart!

Throughout these events, Lil Nas X challenged many of the commonly accepted assumptions about what a musical genre is. He demonstrated that the power to determine who is going to be successful lies in the hands of the consumer and no longer in the hands of a system that for years left artists like him behind.

Lil Nas X is a Gen Zer, and his story might be a blueprint of an emerging Gen Z culture and its potential to significantly transform the broader American culture. It is a story of *radical inclusivity*, *willingness to challenge authority*, and *a new age of creativity* where culture is reinvented and rapidly "trickles up" and becomes accepted by broad audiences, including older generations.

Radical Inclusivity

Growing up as a diverse group where different flavors, opinions, and habits are accepted, respected, and brought together in various forms, Gen Zers have the knowledge, personal experience, and technology to integrate the many strands into a multifaceted culture. A culture that is whole yet allows every part to stand on its own and truly celebrate American diversity. As we saw earlier, for Gen Zers, diversity is a core value and inclusivity, a principle to live by.

David Schmid, an English professor at the University of Buffalo, told me that concepts like inclusivity "have been internalized as common sense by Gen Z." For the students he teaches, "tolerance and acceptance of diverse genders, race, or sexualities are not an issue; no one really debates that anymore." He went on, "Take, for example, feminism. Generation Z would not necessarily identify themselves as feminists, and if you ask them, a lot may even shy away from that term. But in terms of exhibiting the influence of those ideas? Yes, absolutely."

According to Schmid, "Twenty years from now, it's unlikely that members of Gen Z are going to define themselves in singular terms as being either *this* or *that*. It's more likely that they will think of themselves as '*this and that and that and a little bit of that, too*'"—a reflection of Gen Z's disdain for labels and easy categorization and of the radically inclusive culture they are creating.

Radical inclusivity entails more than mere acceptance of others. It is based on the idea that the world is increasingly more complex and that it is neither realistic nor practical to think that there is only one way of doing things. It is about explicitly embracing different, sometimes opposing, points of view, without dismissing any one of them—something that makes the process of connecting to other human experiences both enriching and worthwhile. Radical inclusivity employs a cultural dialogue that is rooted in curiosity, which for Gen Zers extends beyond gender or race issues to the world in a broader sense.

"This generation is more curious than previous generations," Schmid told me. "They are particularly curious about the world. The majority of the students that I teach spend some time abroad during their time in college, and they don't think of themselves as Americans in a narrow sense. They are likely to be much more open to experiencing other cultures and to think of themselves as world citizens. In that regard their cultural literacy is more diverse than it was a generation ago."

Kathy Merlock Jackson, a professor of communications at Virginia Wesleyan University, shared a similar view. "Gen Z looks at the world as a much larger place," she said. "Previous generations were taught more about Western cultures. As that changes, and with the cultural exposure that comes with technology, Gen Z has a greater need to travel to places that were not on the radar screen before. They want to go to Africa, Antarctica, Asia. Because they are exposed to more things, they desire to see something that is very different from their own worlds."

Challenging Authority

Gen Z may not party as hard as previous generations, but they certainly play hard when it comes to challenging authority. Gen Z has demonstrated their willingness to speak up, question the way things are done, launch movements, and change the conversation on any subject from arts to politics. Or as Ashley put it, "We are conscious and aware of what's going on around us, and we are willing to speak up and are not afraid to say what we think."

It all starts with a distrust of institutions.

Though Americans of all stripes distrust traditional institutions, Gen Z's distrust toward government and centralized institutions of power is particularly striking. My research shows that 64 percent of Gen Zers have low trust or no trust in government, and as much as 55 and 58 percent don't trust corporations or mass media, respectively (see Figure 4.1). While these numbers are not too different from those of other generations, Gen Zers, at their young ages, are just as disenchanted as those who have had more life experiences on which to base their distrust.

Figure 4.1. A Trust Crisis

Q: How would you describe the level of trust you have in the following institutions?

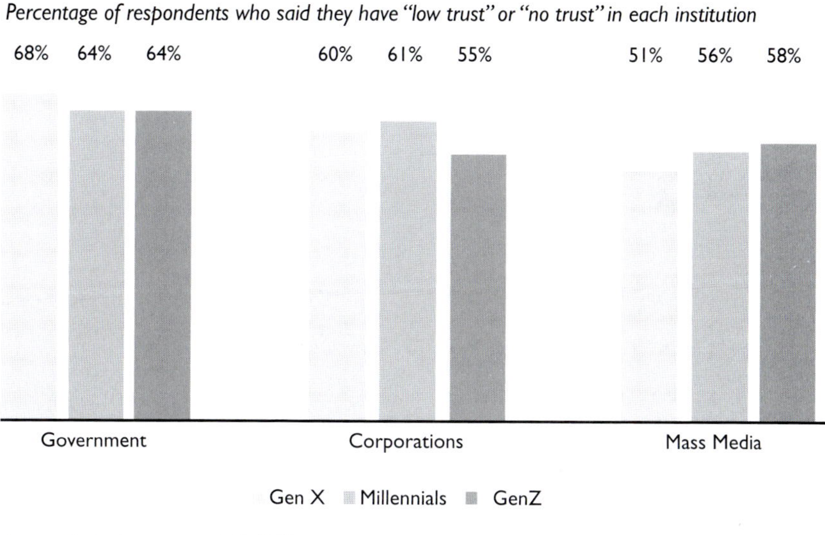

Source: Gen Z Planet research; N=3000

More important is that Gen Zers are not just complaining about these institutions; they are actually taking action. Frustrated with older adults in power who have not tackled tough issues like climate change, gun control, or social injustice, younger Americans are taking matters into their own hands, willing to disrupt the status quo to protect their futures.

Gen Z's interest in these issues stems not from youthful idealism, but rather practical necessity. "Gen Z is the first generation growing up in a situation where some of the problems we face are truly global, and dealing with them individually or even at a national level is not going to cut it," Schmid said. "You need to think in a much broader, more cosmopolitan sense."

Challenges like climate change, wealth inequality, global debt, and recently the coronavirus pandemic gradually foster a culture of "we are in it together" and show the need to collaborate across borders, real or metaphorical, to seek solutions. Successful collaborations require an inclusive mindset, an openness to ideas, and an ability to bring people together.

Being the digital natives, Gen Zers understand the power of digital platforms and how to use them to quickly mobilize large numbers of people toward a goal. "We can create a movement in a moment. We are the generation that was watching from the sidelines for a very long time and we were excluded, but now that many of us are turning eighteen, we have the right to vote and we will be part of the conversation," said Amy. "I think our voices will matter. We are moving from awareness to involvement."

In addition to Parkland high school students and Greta Thunberg, whom I mentioned earlier, many Gen Zers have taken extraordinary actions on various issues. For example, trans activist Jazz Jennings is helping transgender youth to cope by sharing her own struggles and journey to find acceptance. Marley Dias launched a campaign to donate books featuring Black girls as the main characters to other Black girls so they could read about characters they can identify with, and Mari Copeny worked tirelessly to raise awareness of the Flint water crisis.[64]

In an unprecedented case, a group of 21 youth plaintiffs, ages 11 to 23, is suing the U.S. government for its failure to combat climate change. The lawsuit, *Juliana v. United States*, asserts that the government violated the youths' rights for safe life, liberty, and property by allowing activities that harmed the climate. The lawsuit also sought to require the government to adopt methods for reducing carbon dioxide emissions. While previous lawsuits in a similar vein have been dismissed by U.S. courts, the case attracted attention in 2016 when a judge in Oregon upheld the idea that access to a clean environment was a fundamental right, allowing the case to proceed. In January 2020, a Ninth Circuit panel reversed the case, but attorneys for the youth proceeded to appeal the decision. If successful, this case could have far-reaching implications for future generations.[65]

But perhaps the most telltale sign of Gen Zers' sense of responsibility is the high level of volunteer work they perform (see Figure 4.2). More than 55 percent of Gen Zers who participated in my research said they had volunteered at school or in the community over the past year, compared to 38 percent for Millennials and 35 percent for Gen Xers.

Gen Z is creating a culture of social engagement. They define themselves by what they do for the greater good—to the point where they incorporate it into their love lives. A 2019 report by Tinder, the dating app, reveals that Gen Zers were more likely than Millennials to mention causes or missions in their bios. "Gen Z wants a partner, not just to match with, but to march with," the report stated.[66]

Figure 4.2. Volunteering

Q: Have you volunteered in your school or community in the past 12 months?

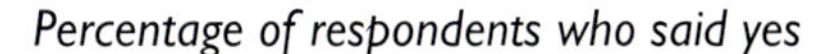

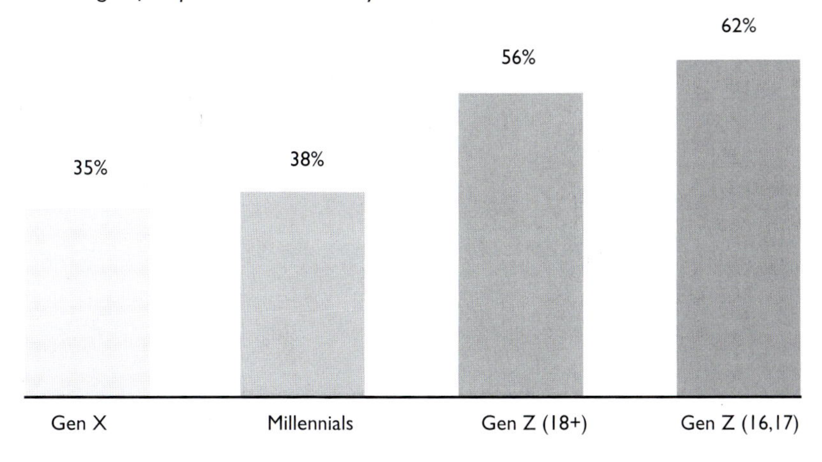

Source: Gen Z Planet research; N=3000

"Getting involved with activism and community—I can say that the frequency and intensity is much greater for my generation," said Jacob, comparing himself to his Millennial siblings and friends. Or as Dylan put it, "We have [a] strong need to 'belong' to something that is bigger than us."

New Age of Creativity

Gen Zers break the rules not only in the social and the political spheres but also in the cultural arena, where their role as culture creators and influencers is already apparent. Professor Jackson of Virginia Wesleyan University said, "This is a generation that wants to be the 'producer-user,' the creator and the audience member at the same time. They don't want to be just the audience. They are the source of the message and the creative force behind the message. This generation is confident in that it sees itself as an active creator, not just passive participant."

This shift from being predominantly consumers of culture to being creators of culture is a profound transition, and one that has the potential to define this generation. With technology at their fingertips, Gen Zers not only have more tools than ever before to create their version of cultural products but also have more venues to easily distribute what they create and see the effects of their creation, almost instantly, through likes, comments, and further sharing.

Shay Rahm is a lecturer at the University of Central Oklahoma who researches popular culture and digital media. In an interview she pointed out that the unique impact of Gen Z on culture lies in their ability to combine ideas, genres, and periods and create a mélange they can call their own:

> Gen Z is using the fact that they are the most diverse and most globally aware generation to cross-pollinate different aspects of

> pop culture. For example, video games that use rap music, or rap music that uses sounds of video games, bilingual or multilingual music, and videos that combine text, music, and images to deliver a message or share their views. They are influenced by people from different countries [think K-pop], and they are layering all these different things one upon another, mixing many genres into one.

Schmid agrees: "More than ever, the culture that is going to be produced by Gen Z will be a combination of things that already exist: nostalgia, kitsch, cynicism, outright criticism. It's in this kind of combination that we are going to see a culture that is going to be more hybrid and more diverse. And while culture always had that hybrid quality, with Gen Z, all the ideas of purity, origin, singularity, and clarity will be thrown out of the window and instead we will have this mélange of influences."

You might say that Gen Z is the ultimate mix-and-match generation, and you have to look no further than Billie Eilish to see that.

With her baggy pants, oversize sweatshirts, whispery voice, and brightly colored hair, Eilish is both feminine and masculine. She seems both distant and intimate, judgmental and empathetic, vulnerable and without pretense, yet forthright and practical. She writes and records her music in her bedroom, shares her life on social media like other teenagers do, and has the maturity to understand that her creations are for her audience to interpret. "One of my favorite parts about making music is that people take it in the way that they take it, and I have no control over that," she told *Hot Ones* host Sean Evans.[67]

In addition to emerging as a successful pop artist, the 18-year-old has become perhaps the quintessential spokesperson for Gen Z in that she defies easy definitions. Her music, which first came to prominence through SoundCloud, is an eclectic mix of pop, electropop, alternative, trap hip-hop, and electronic dance music. She counts as her influences Tyler the Creator, Earl Sweatshirt, Lana Del Ray, and Amy Winehouse as well as the Beatles and Frank Sinatra.[68]

Eilish is not alone in reverting to the past. *Stranger Things,* the Netflix hit mystery show about young kids confronting supernatural forces in an otherwise ordinary town during the 1980s, has become very popular with Gen Zers. So has *Friends,* the popular sitcom that depicted life in New York City in the '90s.

Perhaps they are responding to universal core issues young people deal with—such as family relationships, love, friendships, and jobs—and those have not really changed. Or they might be fascinated with a world that is much simpler than the world they know. One without mobile phones and social media, and where people go to coffee shops to meet friends instead of sitting alone with their laptops and headsets being connected and disconnected at the same time.

In one of my polls on media consumption, Gen Zers seem to agree that it's the latter that captured their hearts and minds. "It is the simplicity and naivety of the past that is appealing to me," wrote one participant. "Everything seems very carefree and more relaxed. Today there's so many rules and issues that young adulthood automatically means heavy responsibilities, there's no time to enjoy being young." Another stated, "I look to the past to find inspiration and comfort. The things that are released today are incredibly overrated."

Gen Z is clearly reverting to the past not out of a single-minded nostalgia but as a way of finding truth and inspiration and as a way of finding content that they can recycle and call their own.

A major reason that Gen Z is so open to the past is that they have easy access to it, especially compared to pre-Internet generations like Gen X and Baby Boomers. Whereas previous generations existed in historical silos, the Internet has allowed Gen Z to unify cultural components that were once unique to a particular era.

"One way that Gen Z artists are going to be different than previous generations is that they have easy access to everything that was ever recorded, and that is going to create a different kind of art," said David Yaffe, a nationally renowned arts critic and assistant professor of humanities in Syracuse University's College of Arts and Sciences. "People my age had to dig through records. If you wanted something, you had to buy it or borrow it. But now, for somebody who is interested in music and wants to know everything there is to know, it is much easier because everything is accessible, and a lot of it is free. For older generations, this is something that is truly difficult to appreciate."

Another area where Gen Z is changing the rules, also thanks to technology, is their clear preference for the visual and the short form.

More than generations before them, Gen Zers have the means to communicate in visual forms, which they find both convenient (one emoji can replace a whole sentence) and satisfying as it allows them to express wide range of emotions and ideas in ways that were not possible before (think a meme or a GIF as a form of cultural critic).

In addition, Gen Z has mastered the art of short-form video clips that last anywhere from a few seconds to a few minutes. While Hollywood has previously experimented with short-form movies and shows for the Internet, Gen Z's preference for mobile devices and streaming content has made the short (or very short) form more of a reality.

Snapchat, understanding the appeal of the short form, has fielded successful short-format shows, including *The Dead Girls Detective Agency,* a series of five-minute episodes in which deceased characters investigate their own murders. Snapchat reported that "14 million unique viewers watched the first season."[69] But perhaps the strongest evidence of the appeal of short-form video is the rapid rise of TikTok, which spectators attribute to Gen Zers, who have turned the platform into a playground of self-expression, creativity, cultural and political criticism, and more.

Gen Zers who responded to my media poll had strong views as to why they prefer short-form media. The main reasons they cited were compatibility with their busy schedule ("I am extremely busy, so short form still lets me have leisure without feeling guilty"), difficulty to focus for long time ("short-form media is great, especially if you have a short attention span"), efficiency ("short form gets faster to the point"), and effectiveness ("short form forces information to be condensed into bite-sized time frames, it is easier to consume because there is not as much fluff"). But they also expressed appreciation of the medium and what it takes to produce it. As one of the participants stated: "What I like about short-form media is how much creative ability you have to have to communicate information or entertainment in a very short time."

Experts predict that the emergence of short-form content will spread to other media formats, including books and music. "Everything is going to get shorter," Kathy Merlock Jackson said. "Obviously, it's hard to read a long thing on a device. So the technology impact is that things are getting more compressed. Gen Z just wants the main points. It's all about the practicality and efficiency."

The music industry, in particular, has long resisted the idea that short-form content can convey any artistic depth. Classic songs like "Hey Jude" by the Beatles and "Bohemian Rhapsody" by Queen run eight and six minutes, respectively. "Maybe songs will be thirty seconds long," Yaffe told me. "Something that gets you right away. Nobody [has] really done that yet. Songs have gone longer but they have not gone shorter—a pop song is typically three minutes. Maybe there could be songs that are equivalent to the video short-form series concept."

Trickle-Up Culture

In early February 2020, the *Today* show team gathered in front of Rockefeller Center in New York City to film a TikTok dance video—a courageous step into Gen Z territory, for better or worse. The highly popular team was well received by enthusiastic TikTokers, who made comments such as "Welcome to TikTok," "you guys did great :)," and "OMG this is awesome," along with "Poor Craig, your effort is appreciated" and "The struggle is real." It was an early sighting of adults on TikTok.

Was it unusual? Not really.

Whatever happens with Gen Z doesn't stay with Gen Z. This is why studying who they are is extremely important. As they adopt new technologies and ideas, their thinking and behaviors trickle up to other generations, having an outsize influence. Members of previous generations have joined Gen Zers in their activism across a wide spectrum of causes. Emojis are used widely by all age groups. Adults are making TikTok videos. The Gen Z mindset is spreading through society, creating opportunities and challenges for educators, employers, and brands. Are you ready?

Chapter 4: The 360 View

Gen Z is set to transform American culture in more than one way. In the past few years, a blueprint of "Gen Z culture" started to emerge, providing us a glimpse into where the culture is heading. This blueprint has three core elements:

- **Radical Inclusivity.** For Gen Z, with their diverse demographics and exposure to the world around them, inclusivity is something that many of them view as natural and desirable. Explicit embrace of differences and curiosity about other human experiences are the basis for what they view as a just society.

- **Willingness to challenge authority.** Gen Zers have demonstrated their willingness to speak up, question the ways things are done, launch movements, and change the conversation on anything from arts to politics. Being the digital natives, Gen Zers understand the power of social platforms and how to use them to quickly mobilize large numbers of people toward a goal.

- **New age of creativity.** Gen Z's role as culture creators and influencers is already apparent. The cultural products they are creating increasingly lie in their ability to combine ideas, genres, and periods and create a mélange they can call their own. They have clear preference for the visual and short form.

Finally, whatever happens with Gen Z doesn't stay with Gen Z. As they adopt new technologies and ideas, their thinking and behaviors trickle up to other generations. They are bringing their culture, core values, strengths, and personal challenges to the workplace and to the consumer market alike, promising to challenge everything we know about culture, work, and commerce.

My Biggest Dream . . .

I want to create something (film, book, whatever) that will have a positive influence on people and give them some form of happiness.

Elise, 20, Pennsylvania

Be a YouTuber and create content about my favorite games.

Benjamin, 17, Massachusetts

Help others, and make the world a better place.

Megan, 17, Washington

Invent something that will change the world.

Diego, 16, Indiana

Become an activist for equal rights.

Spencer, 17, Arkansas

I wish people could get along with each other no matter what race, religion, or color they are.

Dreamer: Ethan, 19, Colorado

Artist: Victoria Fernandez, 36, Madrid, Spain

BAN
HATE

WE STAND
TOGETHER

PART II

Work

CHAPTER 5

Most Educated, Least Prepared?

"**GOOD MORNING, WINNER.** Take a deep breath. Good. You're ready to dominate this day. You've worked harder than everyone, and that is why you're a champion. You understand that greatness takes sacrifice. Visualize what you still want to achieve. Stand atop the mountain of your success and look down at everyone who's ever doubted you. . . ."[70]

This is the mantra that Molly, the intense lead character in the film *Booksmart,* recites each day. She has worked very hard to get top grades so she can attend a prestigious college and get ahead. However, in the process, Molly and her best friend, Amy, missed out on the fun parts of high school, like partying and dating. Worst of all, Molly discovers that Harvard accepted Gigi, a party girl who didn't study nearly as much as the two protagonists.

Was the sacrifice worth it?

That's a question many Gen Zers will probably ask themselves once they enter the professional workforce. From taking AP classes and earning college credits to loading their schedules with extracurricular activities that boost their résumés, most Gen Zers believe they must earn a college degree in order to get a good job and gain financial security. Once in college, they work hard to earn top grades, get as much work experience as they can, and search for that perfect job. However, for many Gen Zers, the education they worked so hard to obtain in high school and college will likely fall short of what the future job market requires.

Thanks to the ever-quickening pace of innovation, once-new technology becomes obsolete fast. Companies and industries once thought indestructible are being challenged. Skills once considered valuable quickly become irrelevant as artificial intelligence, automation, and advanced computing displace them. In its "The Future of Jobs" report, the World Economic Forum argues that this rapid technological change means that "nearly 50 percent of subject knowledge acquired during the first year of a four-year technical degree is outdated by the time students graduate."[71] In an environment where knowledge becomes outdated so quickly, technical skills, while still indispensable for the workplace, are increasingly insufficient. On the other hand, softer skills, like problem solving, creative thinking, collaboration, and communication, are emerging as critical because they allow workers to respond effectively to the fast-changing world around them.

Gen Zers, who were brought up to believe they must study specific subjects like accounting or law, will show up for work highly educated, motivated, and armed with the knowledge they acquired over the years, but they most likely will not possess the full spectrum of these soft skills. Even their positive attitude and their belief that any answer is only a Google search away will not be enough to close the gap. Therefore, the training and integration of Gen Zers into the workforce becomes a business imperative and the responsibility of business leaders.

The Most Educated Generation Ever

Compared to previous generations, Gen Z appears to have the highest levels of academic achievement. They have a lower high school dropout rate (6.4 percent for the first cohort compared to 14 percent for the Millennial's first cohort),[72] and they have the highest college enrollment rate. According to the Pew Research Center, "among those who were no longer in high school in 2017, 59 percent were enrolled in college, higher than the enrollment rate for 18- to 20-year-old Millennials in 2002 (53%) and Gen Xers in 1986 (44%)."[73]

This trend is consistent with my own findings. Eighty-nine percent of Gen Zers who participated in my research and who are currently in high school said they plan on going to college. And among those who are in college, 25 percent believe they will eventually need a graduate degree to succeed in today's market. "Everyone goes to college these days, compared to previous generations," one teenager told me during a focus group in New York. "College education is no longer a differentiating factor."

So, what does make someone stand out? Gen Zers believe the answer is *relevance*.

They grew up during the 2008 recession. They are well aware of the enormous amount of student loan debt that Americans carry and the bleak predictions that robots will replace human workers. Therefore, Gen Zers' view of education is rather pragmatic—it is all about that future job. Alexandra, a 17-year-old from Pennsylvania who juggles her school commitments with work at a convenience store, told me that although her real talent is in art (she is good at drawing and sculpting), she has concluded that "it is not realistic to pursue this talent because I am concerned about the financial viability of being an artist." Instead she plans on going to nursing school.

A Harris Poll found that "two-thirds of 14- to 23-year-old students want a degree to provide financial security, ranking it above all else when it comes to their motivation for going to college."[74] And since

Silicon Valley is a major driver of U.S. economic growth, students want careers in computer science and software design. "Fewer students are majoring in the humanities," education strategist Jeffrey Selingo wrote in the *Washington Post*. "More flock toward science, technology, engineering and math majors—known collectively as STEM—that they think will burnish their employment prospects."[75] In the past decade, the share of STEM degrees conferred in the United States rose from 29 percent to 37 percent.[76]

Yara, the 18-year-old from Illinois who is about to begin her classwork in computer engineering at a university in Chicago, explained why she chose this field of study: "I want to be relevant to the job market once I graduate from college. I want to make sure that my efforts and the financial investment my parents will be making in my education are going to pay off."

Even students who are not enrolled in STEM-related fields are increasingly interested in obtaining certificates in topics like data analytics or artificial intelligence before they graduate—programs that colleges have started to offer in recent years.

Currently enrolled in an Arizona university, Emma, 21 years old, used her time during the coronavirus quarantine months to do just that: "I am taking online certificates in Excel and coding with Columbia and Harvard universities. I'm doing it because I think the university has become the minimum standard. It doesn't set you apart . . . the certificates help me in my job search . . . they [potential employers] always widen their eyes whenever I tell them I am taking classes outside of my university."

But are these students, reared in an education system that trains them to pass standardized exams and master hard skills, truly prepared for the digital economy?

A Shifting Economy and Workforce

Gen Zers will face a workplace that is vastly different from anything Boomers, Xers, and even Millennials have experienced. They are joining the workforce in the midst of a digital revolution, or what the World

Economic Forum termed the Fourth Industrial Revolution. The first two revolutions transformed the world through water, steam, and electric power that enabled mass production. The third was based on the use of electronics and the information technology that drove automation. The Fourth, however, is not a mere incremental change over the last one. "It is characterized by a fusion of technologies that is blurring the lines between the physical, digital, and biological spheres. . . . and it is distinct because of its velocity, scope, and systems impact."[77]

To cope with the depth and breadth of these changes, companies are gradually changing their operating models to reflect the economic forces unleashed by breakthrough technologies like artificial intelligence, 3D printing, or genomic editing. And they have started building the capabilities and the work environments that are required to compete in a world in which innovation is the biggest source of competitive advantage.

Compared to the traditional workplace, which had at its center the highly specialized individual working in a functional silo, the innovation-era workplace is driven by multidisciplinary, multifunctional, and highly connected teams that leverage internal and external resources to innovate. In this new era, teams are encouraged to explore, test new ideas, fail, and learn instead of getting things right the first time. Organization structures and business processes are flexible so companies can effectively respond to change. Career paths are nonlinear, meaning that employees can move up or sideways based on their skills, abilities, and interests. Workers derive job satisfaction because they have a broader sense of purpose that comes from being empowered and connected, as opposed to simply a sense of achievement that comes from completing a task or delivering a project. Companies reward employees who challenge authority and conventional thinking versus those who simply follow the rules. Most important, companies expect employees to be lifelong learners who can adapt to the fast-moving world around them (see Table 5.1). In this brave new world, knowledge is important but not enough. To succeed in a fast-changing world, workers will increasingly need soft skills like complex problem solving, critical thinking, and collaboration.[78]

Table 5.1. Innovation-Era Workplace—Operating Model Shifts

Workplace Characteristics	From	To
Performance unit	Individual	Team
Type of knowledge required	Deep (specialization)	Broad (multidisciplinary)
Desired behaviors	Follow the rules	Break the rules
Learning and development	Event-driven (spot training)	Lifelong learning
Operational philosophy	"Do it right the first time"	Try, fail, learn, repeat
Organization structure/processes	Rigid	Flexible
Value is created through	Standardization	Customization
Career paths	Linear	Nonlinear
Innovation	Internally focused/ Secretive	Externally networked/ Open
Employee engagement is driven by	Sense of achievement	Sense of purpose

Source: Gen Z Planet research

Maeve Coburn, a learning and transformation executive at L'Oréal, told me that the most important skill of the future is *"learning how to learn"*— how quickly one can learn and integrate new knowledge into the day-to-day will make the difference between high and low performers.

The ability to influence others is another important skill on Coburn's list: "The employee of the (near) future is no longer working in a silo. They will have to manage multiple interdependencies inside and outside their immediate work environment, often in areas where they don't have decision authority. As such, being able to build relationships, understand what people's motives are, and being able to influence them will become critical skills." But perhaps the most challenging aspect for newly graduated employees is the fact that organizations and tasks have become more complex. Employees, even at the entry level, will need to operate in the "gray areas" where there are no clear right or wrong answers. And according to Coburn "they will need to make good decisions based on sound judgment and an understanding of tradeoffs and what is at stake."

However, Gen Zers do not feel that they are fully prepared to deal with this new reality. Thirty-six percent of my research participants said they don't feel their education has prepared or is preparing them well for the real world, pointing to gaps in soft skills. Dylan, 19 years old from Illinois, who just completed his first year of college, where he studies software engineering, told me:

> I think school has taught me a lot of the technical skills that I will be using at work, but I don't think that it's possible to learn all of the skills that you need in a classroom environment. You need real experience to learn how to work with others or how business operates. I am aware that my education is not fully preparing me for these situations, so I am doing a lot of learning on my own, reading about leadership and management. Right now I am reading a book by Dale Carnegie called *How to Win Friends and Influence People*. I am learning pretty quickly that the most important skill is how to deal with and how to work with people.

The business world seems to agree. Only 36 percent of business leaders surveyed by the Boston Consulting Group in 2020 believed that educational institutions give their graduates adequate training.[79]

Or as Krista Davis, head of organizational development at the Novartis Pharmaceuticals Corporation (a U.S. affiliate of Novartis AG), told me: "Universities or colleges today are not necessarily preparing their graduates to thrive in today's work environment. They provide them with excellent knowledge and technical skills, but they don't provide them with the life and the behavioral skills that are needed to succeed. . . . It is hard to change institutions that have done things the way they have done it for so many years, but we are more and more seeking to do just that."

Responding to the Skills Gap

In response to the changing workplace, colleges, communities, and businesses around the country are making an effort to close the skills gap. Colleges are rethinking their curriculums. Communities are creating alternative programs to give kids an early start on real-world experience. And businesses are looking to collaborate with educational institutions, influence their curriculum, build relationships with top talent, and develop the capabilities needed to coach newcomers on the skills they deem important.

Colleges, aware of the demand of the workplace, are trying to keep up by offering more flexible programs across multiple disciplines. For example, at Union College in New York, students can earn a Bachelor of Arts *and* a Bachelor of Science degree in five years. "Union education encourages students to explore the creative spaces where ideas intersect and new solutions merge, and it lets them apply those ideas in practical settings," the school's website says. "Drawing connections among the arts, engineering, humanities, science and social sciences, and applying those connections to problem-solving is where our students truly excel."[80]

Yet some schools and communities believe that addressing the skills gap must start long before kids get to college. They view the current education system as too narrowly focused on preparing students for passing standardized tests. Instead, they have created alternatives to prepare kids for the workforce and adult life.

One example is Iowa BIG, a public high school program that partners with local businesses to put teenagers to work on real-world projects. The program's stated mission is "to assist students in developing their agency, efficacy, and passions while gaining valuable real-world and academic skills so they can succeed in a world of rapid and constant change."[81] Trace Pickering, executive director and co-founder of Iowa BIG, shared with me how the program started:

> Following a 2008 flood that almost wiped out half of our downtown, community leaders at Cedar Rapids felt that there was an opportunity to rethink many aspects of the community including education. We sent industry leaders that represented the gamut of industries, backgrounds and beliefs in our community to spend one day in our schools and later discussed with them their observations. The feedback was consistent. They saw bored kids, teachers who worked hard to keep their attention, and it was clear to them that the classroom traditional separation of disciplines de-contextualizes and therefore limits learning.

Armed with this knowledge, the leaders set out to create a program that focuses on people and their passions, connects them to the community, and gives students practical work to do. By working on real-world problems, students can see how various disciplines, like history and government, or biology and industry, relate to each other. The resulting projects include helping a local warehouse to improve its operations, developing a swimming pool alarm system to ensure safety for kids, and using therapy dogs to teach young children about mental illness.

Pickering said the organization is only beginning to evaluate the results, but he thinks the program has been extremely valuable in helping its participants in their college applications and in life in general: "Besides being admitted to colleges, including Ivy League institutions, 88 percent of Iowa BIG graduates feel that they do better in managing time, space, networking and advocating for themselves thanks to their participation in the program. The idea is to develop 21st-century skills at an early stage." Pickering hopes that the model they built will inspire change so that kids can have similar experiences as part of the formal education system: "I will celebrate the day that Iowa BIG is not needed because this is just a part and parcel of what every student should have access to."

Students at High Tech High in San Diego, California, are also shaking things up. The subject of the documentary film *Most Likely to Succeed*, High Tech High, is unique: there are no bells, and the day is not divided up by time periods or subjects. Instead, the school combines subjects through project-based learning. The idea is that learning is best achieved by doing, by encountering challenges and solving complex problems, by owning something from beginning to end, and by having a sense of purpose. In the process, students develop a range of soft skills, including resilience, willingness to try and fail, creativity, and collaboration.

While both communities and colleges are starting to grasp the need for developing 21st-century skills, corporate America, at least in the near to medium term, will have to bear most of the burden of training newcomers and building the skills that are needed for an innovation-era workplace.

Krista Davis of Novartis told me that she sees a more proactive role for corporations, one that goes beyond waiting for recruits to show up and then begin their training: "To close the skills gap, we have to work with colleges, share with the students what's important to us, what are the skills and the behaviors that they are going to need to demonstrate, and help them have a clearer picture of what it takes to be successful in a corporate environment through meaningful exposure to our team and leaders. Furthermore, I would like to see us, and other organizations move toward closer relationships with schools and be able to influence the curriculum in a way that benefits everyone involved."

Julia, 22 years old from California, who recently graduated from college with a degree in horticulture science, would have loved to have a broader curriculum. She feels that her curriculum lacked the subjects and experiences that could have better prepared her for the workplace: "It seems to me that all the classes I took were technical, while being in a workplace is a lot about social skills and soft skills . . . like conflict resolution. . . . I don't think I got any of that unless I was working in a team on a project."

Once newcomers like Julia are at the door, it is up to the employer to build these skills, and according to Davis, it takes more than a training session to do so: "Building behavioral skills requires ongoing coaching. You can't teach in a classroom how to be a good influencer, how to effectively build relationships, or how to adapt your management style. Those skills can only be taught through experience and guidance." To effectively coach, companies need to have clarity about the skills and behaviors they value and the culture they want to foster. For example, Novartis wants workers to be inspired by the company mission, be curious about new ideas that can improve health outcomes for the patients and physicians the company serves, and be "unbossed"—that is, thrive in a culture where leaders are encouraged to empower people to attain their personal and professional goals.

As executives like Davis and others I spoke to are looking to collaborate with higher education institutions and build internal capabilities to close the skills gap, others are taking an entirely different route—hiring young talent without a degree. Apple, Google, Hilton, and Penguin Random House are just a few examples of companies offering well-paid jobs for candidates without a degree.[82] Driven by the belief that a degree doesn't necessarily indicate talent and by the fact that in the current environment many talented individuals cannot afford college education, these companies are looking to develop talent internally, signaling a break from the traditional approach to education and work. This kind of perspective became more prominent during the global pandemic when the spotlight turned to higher education, questioning the value it delivers in light of its high cost, especially when classes must be conducted online. A call for an overall restructuring of the education system sounded loud and clear. Along the same lines, Google launched its "Career Certificate," a six-month program which is promised to be treated as an equivalent to four-year college, perhaps marking the next frontier of tech disruption.

Only time will tell how some of these developments will pan out, but one thing is certain—bringing the next generation of employees onboard during this time of unprecedented change requires not only investment in their training but also an investment in shifting the way an entire organization approaches employee development. For example, if coaching is becoming a part of every manager's job, then everyone needs to learn how to coach—not a small feat. But this is only one aspect of how companies need to change to accommodate the arrival of Generation Z in the workplace. The characteristics and the expectations they bring to the workplace are calling for much more.

Chapter 5: The 360 View

- Compared to previous generations, Gen Z appears to have the highest levels of academic achievement. In recent years, high school dropout rates have declined and college enrollment rates are the highest they have ever been.
- Gen Z views education in a pragmatic way. It's all about that future job. Many are choosing to study science, technology, and engineering—fields where the demand for new workers is high. Those who are not enrolled in STEM-related fields are increasingly interested in obtaining certificates in topics like data analytics or artificial intelligence to improve their job prospects.
- However, Gen Z is joining the workforce in the midst of a digital revolution when companies are busy transforming their operations to ensure that they stay relevant. And while technical skills are extremely valuable in a digital world, soft skills are becoming as important, if not more so. Gen Zers, who were raised in an education system that focused more on hard skills are likely to fall short on these soft skills, placing the burden of closing the skills gap on their future employers.
- Companies can deploy a variety of strategies to help close the skills gap. Collaborating with educational institutions and influencing the curriculum is one approach, but equally effective are building relationships with talent while they are in college and giving them meaningful exposure to the company, its activities, and its leaders. Once they are onboard, companies will have to provide ongoing coaching that focuses on building the desired skills and behaviors to maximize employees' impacts and support their growth.

I wish everyone would stop running around trying to be perfect.

Dreamer: Connor, 16, Connecticut

Artist: Tayfun Pekdemir, 31, Istanbul, Turkey

CHAPTER 6

Gen Z Employees—A World of Opposites

SAMANTHA IS A fashionista. Since she was a child, she has liked dressing up, shopping for clothes, following trends on Instagram, and never wearing the same outfit for school. So when she went to college, selecting a fashion, merchandising, and design major was a natural choice. Samantha thrived as a student and even had a side hustle helping people to resell their clothes online on platforms like Poshmark, for which she received a fee every time an item is sold. "You can't just put items on these platforms," she said, "you must style them correctly, and that takes a skill."

Then came the time to start looking for a "real" job. Samantha, like others in her class, frequented the career center in her school, attended career fairs, took a job seminar that taught her how to update her online profiles and cover letters, and started applying for jobs. LinkedIn and Indeed were her go-to sites to find and apply for positions, and Glassdoor was her main site to find information about companies. "Before applying I want to know as much information as possible about the company culture. It is important to me that I work in an environment that has positive reviews and to know I am going to get along with people," she said. Compensation and benefits were other attributes on her list including 401(k), medical, and paid time off. "After four years in college, I am in a mode of 'save, save, save,' and if an employer is willing to put it aside for me and match it—it helps my savings plan. With everything that is happening today, I can't count on government money [Social Security] later in life. I better take control now."

Another of Samantha's requirements was to stay away from fast-fashion brands because of their negative impact on the environment—"all this crazy amount of clothes that are being made over and over again and no one buying them. . . . I don't want to be part of that." Instead she looked to join a brand that is focused on customers and on creating fashion that is needed in the moment.

Samantha's first foray into full-time employment was less than smooth, though: "Submitting an application online and never hearing back was quite common and very discouraging. There are hundreds of applicants for every job, and companies are not doing a good job in responding." Eventually, Samantha did hear back from a fashion brand she applied to. She had a couple of video interviews and one in-person, after which she was offered a position as a stylist. The process took a long four months, but she was "soooo happy . . . it felt like a dream come true."

But Samantha was up for a disappointment:

> They [her employer] presented themselves as the most amazing brand in the world. They sent me the most exciting job description, and they constantly e-mailed me. . .literally saying "we want you" with exclamation marks, but when I joined, nothing was like what they promised. I was happy to work hard, but the hours were much longer than I expected. . . .

> I worked alone despite them promising me that I will never work alone. . . . I had no support . . . my manager was not so nice . . . and I just felt, "What did I get myself into?"

Samantha, who felt misled, left after three months and found another job as an assistant store manager for a high-end fashion retailer where she is happier. Her first employer not only lost her talent and brand advocacy but also all the costs they incurred recruiting her and having to find a replacement three months later.

Samantha's story is just one of many stories I heard from Gen Zers who recently graduated from college and started their career journeys. The stories have one common thread—they highlight how a new generation of employees with a different set of expectations and behaviors is about to change everything we know about the workplace and how the "war for talent" will intensify.

As we saw in the previous chapter, Gen Z is entering the workforce at a time of unprecedented change. Companies of all types and sizes are transforming their business models, go-to-market strategies, and skills and capabilities to ensure long-term viability in the face of technological disruption and most recently a global health crisis. At the same time, Baby Boomers are exiting the workforce in unprecedented numbers. According to the Pew Research Center, ten thousand Boomers in the U.S. have reached the age of 65 every day since 2011,[83] a trend that will continue till 2030 when the last cohort of the Boomers generation will reach that retirement age threshold. Combined, these two trends—an increased need for digital-economy skills and Boomers exiting the workforce—mean that recruiters are competing fiercely for talent, and many look forward to the promise that a new generation of employees might bring.

While the early cohorts of Gen Z are facing a difficult job market because of the COVID-19 pandemic, they are still expected to account for nearly a third of the U.S. workforce by 2030,[84] so their importance cannot be overstated. After all, the future success of many organizations will depend on their ability to attract, develop, integrate, and retain the next generation of employees.

For their part, Gen Zers seem highly enthusiastic about joining the workforce. They may not have the full spectrum of skills that employers desire, but they do possess behaviors and expectations that promise to challenge and benefit the workplace. Some of these expectations, especially around employer benefits or promotion opportunities, are not significantly different than those of their older counterparts but they appear to place greater value on professional development, diversity, and workplace flexibility (see Figure 6.1).

Throughout my research, Gen Z employees have emerged as a multidimensional group of individuals with three sets of seemingly contradictory characteristics. To start with, Gen Zers are the "high-tech kids" who can easily navigate the Internet to accomplish complex tasks like writing a code or launching a movement, but they are also high-touch individuals who require close supervision and regular feedback. They are independent and entrepreneurial young people who would rather work on their own and have the freedom to shape their assignments, yet they crave community and a sense of belonging. And while idealism and activism have become their hallmarks, they adopt a highly realistic and pragmatic approach to their careers and professional goals.

This chapter will examine these three sets of "opposites" that make Gen Z such a unique group of employees.

Figure 6.1. Workplace Expectations

Q: How important are the following job attributes to you when considering an employer?

Percentage of respondents who said "important" or "extremely important"
(Attributes are ranked by order of importance to Generation Z.)

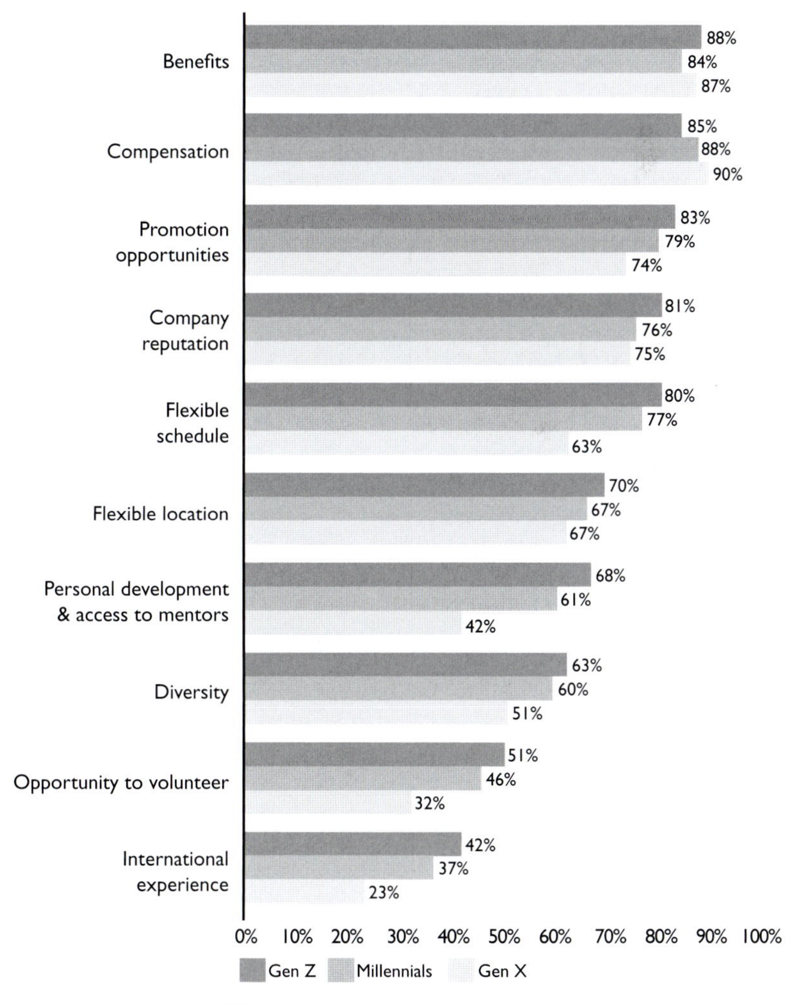

Source: Gen Z Planet research; N=3000

High Tech *and* High Touch

Being the true digital natives, Gen Z enters the workforce with a mindset shaped by years of using mobile devices, applications, and social media networks. Not surprisingly, various studies have found that technology plays a central role in Gen Z's career plans and aspirations. For example, Dell Technologies, in a global survey of twelve thousand Gen Zers, found that 80 percent of Gen Zers "aspire to work with cutting-edge technology,"[85] and 91 percent say "technology would influence [their] job choice among similar employment offers."[86]

Across all generations, any assessment of a potential employer is likely to start online. But Gen Zers, in addition to attending career fairs, checking in with college career centers, and learning the art of networking, will go to great lengths to form an accurate picture of a company from multiple sources: the company website, news reports, stock market performance, social media channels, and third-party review sites. "I always check what people say in the reviews. Glassdoor and Indeed are my main sites," said Alyssa, 20 years old from Michigan, who is in her last year in college studying criminal justice. "A company's website is also important. If a company is not making an effort to communicate clearly who they are and why someone would work for them, why should anyone make an effort to apply?"

You might think that offering an effective recruiting website would be table stakes. Yet a survey from talent acquisition platform Yello found that "63 percent of HR professionals said that their website doesn't adequately show their employee journey or help to attract candidates."[87] So for companies with a website that is not up to snuff, it might be a good place to start. In addition, with young candidates checking every source of information they can find, companies will benefit from ensuring that their employer brand is communicated in a consistent manner across all their digital channels and that they have reviews to match. If you are in a position to do so, ask your employees to write reviews and give candidates a glimpse into your internal culture and practices. Remember, reviews can make or break a job search process.

While having well-designed information channels is important, it is only part of what a company needs to attract the next generation of talent.

Gen Zers want an easy, technology-driven, fast application process, and they have little tolerance for companies that have not adapted to the times. The same report from Yello found that "54 percent of Gen Z candidates won't even submit an application if they think the company's recruiting methods are outdated."[88] And according to another report by iCIMS, a leading provider of talent acquisition solutions, "45% of college seniors would begin considering other jobs if they hadn't received a response from a company within a week after a job interview."[89]

Indeed, for Gen Zers, the application process is all about *control* and *speed.*

Leading companies are responding to these needs by using mobile-based job applications to stand out from competitors and attract talented candidates. Features like interview-scheduling tools that put candidates in control of the timing, video résumés that allow them to present themselves in an authentic way, video interviews that save travel time and costs, and social recruitment are just a few examples of how the field is changing. Amazon, for example, placed a job ad on the popular dating app Tinder. Instead of a dating profile, viewers saw a notice from Amazon Web Services that was listed as "Amazonian." Just as they would do to connect with a potential mate, users could swipe right to demonstrate their interest in the position.[90] Another example is McDonald's. The company began using the photo-sharing app Snapchat to recruit young talent in the summer of 2017. Since many of the chain's applicants are 24 years old and younger, the company sought to meet its potential workers where they spend much of their time—on their phones. Snapchat users, served with 10-second video ads, could watch some of the chain's employees sharing their experiences of working at McDonald's. If interested, a quick swipe will direct them to the company's career site.[91] But mass recruiters like McDonald's or Amazon are not the only companies choosing these approaches. Even more traditional organizations like investment banking giant Goldman Sachs have used Snapchat to recruit college students and better resonate with a new generation of candidates who might be more interested in tech than they are in finance.[92]

Still, not every company is Amazon or Goldman Sachs.

Nathan Candaner, CEO of JobzMall, told me that when considering the broader market, "most companies today, despite the advancements in recruiting technologies, are not well equipped to meet the needs and expectations of this tech-savvy generation." His company, which connects young job seekers to employers, is working to close some major gaps, or as he called them "market disconnects" in serving Gen Z. First, he pointed out that the traditional way of applying for a job has remained largely unchanged, which is neither appealing to Gen Z nor does them a justice. Gen Zers who have become accustomed to shop with one click, write 280-character tweets, and communicate complex ideas in short videos, are expected to read lengthy job descriptions and respond with an equally lengthy document—a résumé, or even worse, a time-consuming online application. Candaner noted that for a 21-year-old student who has limited work experience, the résumé is a limiting medium, not to mention that a résumé can be written by a résumé expert and not the applicant themselves. By contrast, a video résumé allows Gen Z candidates to truly convey who they are, be themselves, and focus on their strengths and what they bring to the table instead of listing every class or internship they have completed. It also gives potential employers a better sense of the candidate's communication skills, personality, and overall presence.

Second, Candaner pointed to a gap in information. The way the recruitment world works does not allow Gen Zers to be fully informed about the range of career opportunities that are available to them. Young people tend be interested in high-profile technology companies or consumer brands with which they are familiar in their daily lives, but they are not aware of the large number of opportunities that may exist in companies that are less visible. "Not everyone is Google or Facebook… ninety percent of the labor force is made up of smaller firms." The same is true for industries. There are no tools today that explain the nature of an industry to candidates, and job boards typically do not provide this information: "In the age of feeds that are dictated by algorithms and targeted advertisement, it's very hard for someone to truly explore."

Understanding these deficiencies, Candaner designed the JobzMall platform as a virtual shopping mall (in some ways, for Gen Z, a job search is not that different from online shopping). The "mall" has digital buildings hosting digital floors that are populated by various industries and companies. The platform enables "job shoppers" to more easily explore and find information that otherwise they would have not been exposed to. According to Candaner, "Candidates who spent time learning about an industry before they apply are 'interested' candidates, and they are more likely to go through the full process and convert compared to random applicants." In addition, job seekers and recruiters are given video tools to present themselves to each other in a more humane and authentic way. Or as stated on JobzMall home page: "Let's be real. It's the 2020's. Stop applying jobs like it's the 1920's."

Technology is increasingly being used in other stages of the recruiting process as well. From video interviews to ongoing communication with candidates, leading companies are constantly adding new tools that help them appeal to employees who manage every aspect of their lives through clicks and swipes.

Instagram as a New Language

Expecting similarities to their everyday lives does not stop in the recruiting process. Gen Zers believe that work itself should more closely resemble aspects of their personal lives. One main example is the way they communicate. As I discussed earlier, Gen Zers grew up with Instagram, Snapchat, memes, and emojis and thus have formed a distinctly visual style of communication.

David Schmid of the University of Buffalo told me that Gen Z's visual literacy represents the biggest cultural difference between them and previous generations. "This is a generation that has grown up with the Internet, and as a consequence the way in which they communicate with each other and with other people is very different. There is a clear shift from the written to the visual"—and this shift requires different approaches in both teaching and training.

"As an educator," Schmid added, "I have to use visual aids in my teaching much more today than I had [to] twenty years ago. I can't give a fifty-minute lecture without visual aids because that's how Gen Zers process information. So it's about using visuals as a form to access more traditional literacy. Whether you are a teacher or a company, how you communicate with this generation will have to change."

The impact of this phenomenon on how employee training is delivered is significant. Gone are the days when hours of classroom lectures and big folders with PowerPoint printouts formed the core of corporate training. In my research, 46 percent of Gen Zers said they learn more effectively by researching topics online and by watching videos. Therefore, Gen Z will do better with training methods like "microlearning," a teaching style that involves short bursts of content that are delivered in an interactive manner and allow the trainee to choose the pace and amount of learning. As with other emerging HR technology solutions, this one is constantly evolving with the use of augmented reality (AR), virtual reality (VR), and gamification features that seek to create more engaging learning experiences.

Beyond training, Gen Z's inclination toward the visual is poised to significantly impact the way people communicate in the workplace. For many of us who live and die by e-mails, it might be hard to imagine a world without plain text. In the business world, people consider well-written words to carry more weight and professionalism than visuals. But faced with a deluge of information that hinders workplace efficiency and effectiveness, companies have started to look for new ways to communicate and share information. These ways include videos and other visual communication methods. For Gen Z this is all perfectly natural. Why use words where a picture or a video could make a greater impact?

Gen Z's relationship with visual communication runs deeper than the images themselves. Visuals have emerged as a new personal language, a way for Gen Zers to express their emotions, bring their true selves to a situation, and make the communication more personal. A study by Adobe on emoji trends found that "61 percent of Emoji users say they use it at work, most frequently with people at their level. When Emojis are used at work, the majority of the users felt it positively impacts likeability and credibility and makes good news or feedback more sincere."[93]

Wendy, a 22-year-old from Maryland, who graduated with a degree in computer science and landed a job at a national bank, feels that there is some way to go before emojis will be an acceptable form of communication at her relatively conservative work environment. "I do use emojis sometimes, but the person I communicate most with is my mentor, and he is kind of a serious guy. . . . I would love if we get more comfortable using emojis with my team."

Adopting more visual communication doesn't just mean accommodating the preferences of the next generation and making them feel comfortable at work. It can also drive productivity improvement and engagement across an entire company. A global study by TechSmith, a company focused on visual communication, tested the effectiveness of visual vs. nonvisual communication. As the findings on visual communication showed, "Not only do people absorb the information better, they also do so faster. Visual content increases comprehension and accuracy of recall."[94]

Quantifying the potential benefits, the study found that "using visual communications in the right moments could have a substantial impact on business performance, gaining more than $1,700 in productivity for every [U.S.] employee who consumes information as part of their role."[95] This is not surprising, considering the increasing amount of information that is shared every day among employees and the time required to read it, process it, and respond—something that affects both employee engagement and motivation. Younger employees were two times more likely than older generations to want more visual content in workplace communications.[96]

One of my polls of Gen Z confirms these findings. Gen Zers have a positive view of visual communication. "It makes the workplace more personal and friendly," "It can be handy in real-time situations like video conferencing," "It's faster and more convenient." These were just a few of the statements shared by participants about the use of visuals in the workplace. However, they do understand that visuals can sometimes be misinterpreted as unprofessional by older colleagues who are not as accustomed to it. Therefore, visuals should be used only when the context is right. Gen Zers also had a word of caution about the use of videos, pointing out that those that are not kept short enough may turn out to be more time-consuming than e-mails, defeating the case for productivity.

The good news is that adopting more visual communication is relatively easy. It requires first and foremost management decision and support and then the adoption of simple tools like image libraries or video capabilities—minor investments for a potentially high return. Using visuals, as the study shows, not only drives productivity but also promotes creativity and increases engagement, all while resonating with the next generation.

Social Media Culture Comes to the Office

As social media has become an integral part of people's lives, companies have started to realize that they can harness "social media culture" to improve how work is being executed. By using platforms like Slack or Google Hangout, companies hope to boost efficiency and enhance collaboration, allowing people with the right skills and expertise, no matter their location, to instantly access the information they need, communicate, and collaborate to get the work done.

The vision for these types of platforms has been around for at least twenty years but failed to catch on because the technology itself was not mature enough, and many employees were resistant to change. By now, however, the technology is evolving rapidly and is user-friendly, and Gen Z is arriving at the scene. For them, collaboration platforms are not only natural but also desirable. Using them is no different from the way they worked together while in college, sharing information and communicating over social media networks, private WhatsApp groups, and the like.

Brandon, a 22-year-old from Virginia, who graduated in the midst of the pandemic with a psychology degree and is now working as a counselor for a nonprofit organization, was pleased to find out that long memos and high-volume e-mails are not how his organization rolls. Instead, he said, "We are using GroupMe, a mobile messaging app that is used every time we need to inform the entire staff on important things and get people to weigh in. Its short, quick, and on the go."

Daniel Jackson, a director of enterprise technology at Crestron, a provider of office technology solutions, told me that "companies are increasingly adopting technologies that we used to see in retail or other consumer applications, like digital signage, to enhance their internal branding and create a sense of connectivity and community." He believes that much of the office technology that we are seeing today would have been adopted anyway, but the acceleration in adoption is significantly influenced by the increase in the number of younger people in the workplace, starting with the Millennials. Jackson expects that Gen Z will further accelerate the adoption because of their high expectations for technology in the workplace and their willingness to try and use new tech. "Gen Z is by far more adaptable than previous generations regarding technology, and they would end up driving the technology adoption within the workforce," he said—a point that executives have to consider when they design entry-level roles for the next generation.

Beyond getting their jobs done, Gen Z can play an important role in helping define and facilitate enterprise-wide technology adoption through reverse mentoring or by taking specific roles that allow them to lead in areas where they have digital knowledge and experience.

But They Are Also High Touch. . . .

If you think that the more technologies you adopt, the more you appeal to Gen Z talent, think again. Conflating Gen Z's desire for technology-driven processes with a full automation of those processes could easily become a turnoff!

Wendy, who has a degree in computer science, told me that the first step in her recruiting process with a well-regarded national bank was a video interview during which she was presented with a few questions on a screen, given 30 seconds to think of her answers, and then given additional time to record them. While being extremely comfortable with technology, she was a bit disappointed not to have a face-to-face interview (on video, of course) with her future employer: "I honestly understand why they are doing it this way. There are so many applicants, and this was just a screener . . . but I'd rather speak to a real person."

Despite their dependency on technology in every aspect of life and work, Gen Zers like Wendy still desire a personal connection. In fact, they want so much of it, you would say they are "high touch." Therefore, companies will have to adopt more personal approaches when recruiting, interacting with, directing, and offering feedback to Gen Zers, and that requires much more than simply finding a balance between human interactions and machine interactions.

Christine Waddick, assistant vice president of organization development and talent at Sun Life Canada, shared with me how Sun Life made their recruiting process more personal to these candidates:

> We used to go to campuses in a very traditional way with a formal presentation that described our organization and the potential journey for college graduates, but that doesn't work anymore. Over the past few years, we learned that personal connection and storytelling are extremely important to attract the next generation of employees. They want to hear directly from our leaders and from current employees who went through our programs about their experience and the opportunities that were available to them when they joined. They look for authenticity and honesty, and companies will have to figure out ways to deliver that authenticity in person on campus and on their various online channels.

The need for personal connection increases once Gen Zers are onboard. Robert Half International, the staffing and HR consulting firm, stated in a report on the future of work that "74 percent of Gen Zers prefer to communicate face to face with their colleagues at work."[97] In addition, my own research shows that 45 percent of Gen Zers feel they work best when they work on their own but require detailed guidance from their managers. This is compared to 36 percent of Millennials and 22 percent of Gen Xers who said the same.

"I prefer to have detailed and hands-on guidance from my manager, at least [in] the early days," said Dylan, the software engineering student. "This will make me feel more comfortable with what I am doing, but as time goes on, I would like to have some freedom." Emily, the psychology student from New York, echoed Dylan's view: "I prefer to get detailed guidance. I am a very detail-oriented person. I just need to know exactly what my boss needs from me."

Maeve Coburn of L'Oréal told me that it is increasingly common to see newcomers who "on one hand want freedom to shape their daily work and seek meaningful responsibility, while on the other hand they feel they need close guidance or a checklist that they can execute against." She attributes these seemingly contradictory expectations to the increasing complexity of the workplace and the complexity of the tasks that need to be performed. According to Coburn, success lies in employers' ability to offer a new kind of onboarding experience that goes beyond the traditional introduction to the company: "New employees need to be introduced to the context of their work, the organization's ways of working and the interdependencies between functions, and be supported in navigating these complexities."

In addition to close guidance, Gen Zers want frequent feedback.

Wendy loved it when she joined her bank and had biweekly review sessions with her manager: "It was focused on my performance but also if I had any questions . . . or just general conversation about our team." However, with the outbreak of the global pandemic and the move to work from home, the frequency of these sessions declined, "which made it really hard. . . . I would like to have at least monthly sessions to make sure I am doing okay." Emily echoed a similar sentiment: "I need to know what my boss thinks about my work at every step of the process, how can I improve, and what I need to do to meet or exceed expectations." Indeed, Gen Zers want feedback early and often.

In many leading organizations, the process of feedback has been a top-of-mind issue for executives. Maeve Coburn of L'Oréal views feedback and reviews as key processes that companies will need to overhaul in the future in order to meet the expectations of the next generation and develop talent that is fit for a 21st-century workplace. "Management in general will have to move from *control-and-manage* to *coach-and-develop*," she said. "There is a need to humanize the process and focus on individual development and not only on hard performance measures."

Barbra Katz, chief human resources officer at Crum & Forster, agrees: "The performance review is evolving beyond the top-down or even the two-way conversation that it used to be. It has become more about a 360-degree, information-rich process where we look at the employee through the lens of peers and other co-workers and really understand many angles of performance. This is how we translate 'social' into the workplace. We are moving toward a frequent or even constant dialogue instead of once-a-year check-in."

Independent *and* Dependent

Years of access to unlimited amounts of information have shaped Gen Z's learning abilities in an unprecedented way. They became accustomed to independently finding answers to their questions and teaching themselves new skills. Watching YouTube videos, they figured out everything from how to replace a car tire to how to invest in the stock market. They used online access to prepare for exams or find their way in a new city, and they don't see any reason why they can't do the same at work.

This attitude and the ability to find and process large amounts of information can be valuable to employers. Gen Zers can spot trends early, discover competitive activity that has gone undetected, or connect the dots that others have missed. Yet being able to find information and have knowledge doesn't always mean that Gen Zers know how to apply it. And while employers don't want to curb the enthusiasm that comes with independent discovery, it is important that, as part of an ongoing feedback, they provide the coaching and direction that are needed to transition from knowledge to synthesis to application.

But Gen Zers' independent nature goes beyond their natural knack for sifting through information and learning new things. They also possess an entrepreneurial spirit like no recent generation before them. According to a multigenerational survey by Monster.com, 76 percent of Gen Zers believe "they are the owners of their careers and will drive their own professional advancement," compared to 64 percent of Millennials and 67 percent of Gen X.[98] Highly ambitious, they want to make progress quickly and have the desire to work hard for it. "Gen Zers expect to roll up their sleeves, and earn their cash through hard work, dedication and a 'whatever it takes' attitude," said the Monster.com report.[99] Add to that their curiosity, their signature fear of missing out, and a desire to not be "placed in a box," and you get a new breed of employees who are interested in expanding their role beyond its original definition, in taking on more responsibilities, and in seeking opportunities for growth.

Evan, who is technically on the border between Millennials and Gen Z, graduated with a degree in chemical engineering and is now working for a biotech company in New York. He told me that once he got comfortable with his role, he started asking his boss for extra responsibilities. "Doing extra projects helps me to expand my knowledge and challenge myself while working on something by my own," he said. "It also allows me to get exposure to other people in the organization that otherwise I would not interact with. . . . Demonstrating that I can take more responsibilities and showing that I can deliver something on my own will help me move up or get other roles I am interested in." In addition, Evan said, "I see other people in my age group in my company who are doing the same. We are all trying to make a mark and make a name for ourselves. We want to stand out, we want to keep learning."

Nothing could be more appealing to an employer than hiring a group of entrepreneurial natural learners. Lifelong learning is one of the most desirable skills of today's workforce, and exploration and initiative are the foundations of innovation. Yet most companies don't offer entry-level jobs with the kind of flexibility and independence that Gen Zers want. That lack could make their engagement and retention challenging.

The traditional entry-level role was designed as a training platform for a future career with the organization. Employees did relatively simple tasks as they gained experience and eventually advanced. But to keep up with Gen Z, companies may need to rethink the way they staff and train new employees. Some of the human resources executives I spoke to mentioned rotations as an important vehicle to keep Gen Zers challenged and engaged. And while job rotation is not a new concept, it may have significant benefits in the current climate, as it addresses Gen Z's need to constantly learn and evolve and the employer's need to have 21st-century workers who have a broad set of competencies and a better understanding of the various moving parts of their organization.

Wendong Li, a leading expert in organizational behavior who is currently teaching at China University in Hong Kong, told me that it is less about the specific role and more about how companies allow their employees to shape their work: "To meet Gen Z's desire for a high level of job autonomy, companies should empower them from the get-go. Leaders must allow the employee to ask questions, challenge, and participate in the decision-making process related to the task they have to perform. It's not the typical leader-follower instructive style that most of us grew up with, but more of a coaching and collaborative style."

Yet doing so comes with its own challenges.

Daniel Robison, a senior vice president of human resources at Loblaw, Canada's largest grocery retailer, told me that he believes that Gen Z's aspirations for autonomy and participation will be difficult for many organizations to handle:

> Gen Zers are more idealistic and less jaded than previous generations. That idealistic nature means that they can offer companies a fresh perspective because they are more willing to challenge the status quo. When they ask, "Why we are doing something this way and not another," they are not going to accept answers like "Because that's how it was done before." It's a strength that they have, but it's going to be a challenge to the workplace. . . . It will force leaders and managers to think carefully about the "why." Why are you coming to work every day, why things are done one way and not another?

Not being able to provide the "why" certainly makes it difficult to Gen Zers. Samantha, who had a rough start for her career in fashion, shared her frustration: "My company is super-organized. As a national retailer, all our processes and procedures are well documented and I have clear idea about what I have to do each day, but I have no idea why. Why am I printing this report? Why do I have to send certain information to corporate? There's never an explanation behind the request, so I start asking questions because none of it makes any sense to me." Or, as Robison summed it up, "Without being able to tell Gen Zers the 'why', their engagement will be hampered."

In addition to their desire to be empowered and to be in control of their work, Gen Zers have also strong preferences as to where and when the work is done. They treasure hyper-flexibility. Seventy percent of Gen Zers who participated in my research said that location flexibility is an important feature when considering an employer, and 80 percent ranked schedule flexibility as a high priority. These figures were higher than for Millennials and Gen X (see Figure 6.1). The importance of hyper-flexibility is still another indication of Gen Z's desire to work independently on their own time from a place of their choice, assuming the required technology can keep them connected. This preference will be served well in a post-coronavirus world, as many companies have already indicated that working remotely may become the standard way of working.

Yet these preferences don't mean that the physical office is entirely dead. Gen Zers, among others, still want social interaction. "I don't find working from home every day very compelling," Emily said. "I don't think I feel much purpose being at home all day, every day. I need to be around people at least part of the time."

Unlike their predecessors, Gen Z does not expect office perks like ping pong, pool tables, or bean bag chairs. While companies had previously focused on creating collaborative open spaces for Millennials, the trend is swinging back toward private work areas. Research suggests that "Benching is not what Gen Z want; The open office will likely revert back to a micro-privacy environment. . . .

Assigned seating will come back too as Gen Z workers want their own personalized space."[100]

While independence has many positive aspects, it also has drawbacks. "Gen Zers are not as collaborative as the Millennials, who were very team-oriented, wanted to be treated the same, be compensated the same, and feel equal," Christine Waddick of Sun Life Canada told me. "Gen Z is not as much about collaboration as they are about standing out, and this is an area where they will need help. They will need to learn that there is only so much you can achieve as an individual person no matter how good you are or even if you are exceeding expectations in the role. If you don't have a network around you, you will only go so far."

But They Are Also Dependent. . . .

Despite their independent nature, Gen Z possess a deep need to belong and be part of a group. "The main value of my generation is community," said Dylan. "We have a strong need to belong. Having a strong community around us is going to be very important."

Gen Zers desire a work environment that promotes community, connection, and support. Forty-six percent of my research participants said that their ideal working environment would be a small or medium-size enterprise, where they are more likely to find such a work environment. By contrast, only 31 percent said they preferred a large or global corporation—a figure that has serious implications for large organizations (see Figure 6.2).

Figure 6.2. The Ideal Workplace

Q: Which of the following do you consider to be the ideal working environment for you?

Percentage of Gen Z respondents

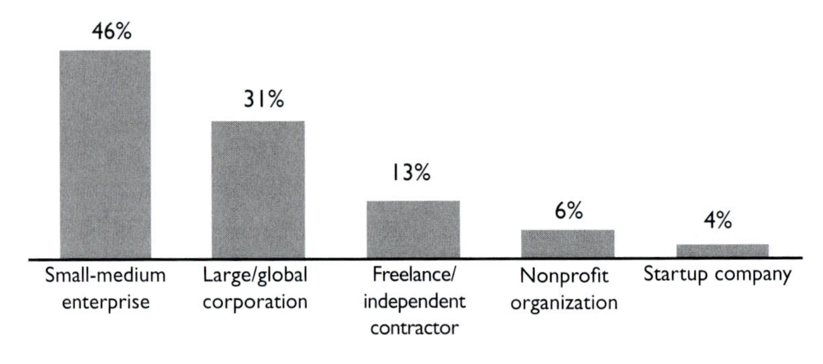

Source: Gen Z Planet research; N=1000

Professor Wendong Li told me that creating a sense of community resides mostly in leadership behavior and their ability to display compassionate leadership style. Compassionate leaders, according to Li, "convey that they truly care about people, their well-being, and their long-term growth and give them what they need to succeed and find purpose in what they do." This is in essence what Gen Z is looking for.

A study by the Workforce Institute found that trust, support, and care are the top three leadership traits Gen Zers seek to have in their managers. "They're looking for leaders who will help them to be inspired in their day-to-day work while encouraging them to try new things and develop professionally over time."[101] Or as Brandon said: "A good leader is someone who is present . . . [someone] who is able to sympathize with his staff and bring people together… who can truly listen . . . keeps the door open . . . and leads by example."

Finding inspiration and meaning at work was a topic that came up often in my conversations with Gen Zers, especially those who are currently in college. Dylan felt that without knowing that his work would have an impact in the world, he can't see how he could do the job. "In order to be truly passionate about what you are doing, you ought to feel that it's worthwhile; otherwise, you will not be giving 100% of yourself." Emily shared a similar sentiment: "Meaningful work is most important. I don't want to be at a desk bored out of my mind every day. I want to love what I do. I want to feel that I am making a difference and be proud of my work."

Gen Z's desire for community and connection means that they prize the kind of stability that comes with longer tenure and company loyalty. Compared to their Millennial predecessors, who preferred short tenures and job hopping, my research shows that 30 percent of Gen Zers would prefer to stay long-term with a company (5+ years) performing one role, while 34 percent said they would like to stay long-term but have multiple roles and experiences. Only 13 percent said they would rather switch from one company to another every few years.

So what drives loyalty?

Door of Clubs, a platform that connects student clubs with potential employers, conducted a survey of Gen Zers that found that empowering work culture was the top reason why they would stay at a job for more than three years, with "high salary raises falling significantly behind." By contrast, another report in 2016 found that for Millennials "high salary was the biggest factor in their loyalty."[102]

Millennials used job hopping to improve their income with every move in order to compensate for the initial low pay they accepted when joining the workforce during the 2008 recession. This acts as a caution to employers who are seeking to incorporate Gen Z into the workforce in what is expected to be a recessionary period after COVID-19. Companies should carefully consider whether compromising entry-level compensation in the short term is worth it, considering the potential benefit of gaining Gen Z's long-term loyalty. Gen Zers are eager to stay longer in the organization. If we find ways to make it work for them by meeting their expectations, it will be a win-win.

Idealistic *and* Realistic

> I want to work for a company that is trying to do something good in the world or in society, in addition to making a profit. A company that embraces people from different backgrounds and with different views. I will not accept a job offer from any company that doesn't meet these criteria even if they pay well. . . . I will feel like a better person following what I believe in.

This is the passionate statement that Sarah, 18-year-old high school student from Georgia, shared with me. It is a good representation of how Gen Z is thinking about which companies they want to work for.

Being committed to bringing about social change, Gen Zers expect their employers to demonstrate that they care, too. Companies must learn how to accommodate Gen Z's activism or risk losing top talent. And they need to be sincere about their efforts. "If a company says that it stands for something, but it doesn't act accordingly, it will be hard for me to buy their story," said Sarah, indicating that companies will gain the trust of Gen Z only if they demonstrate their commitment through actions. Gen Zers expect much more than a few statements in an annual report or the occasional tweet. They want to see companies walk the talk, internally and externally.

Being the most diverse generation, Gen Zers especially value and expect diversity and inclusion in the workplace. My research shows that 63 percent of Gen Zers rated diversity as "important" or "very important" when choosing an employer. This figure was slightly above Millennials (60 percent) and much higher than Gen X (51 percent).

"I want to work in a diverse environment; I want to work in a place where there are more people of color, so I don't feel that I am the only one, as I often felt in my college," said Alyssa, who is African American. "People get very careful around me . . . walking on eggshells . . . being politically correct. . . . I am very interested in race relations and very passionate about what we can do to improve that in the workplace and will look to contribute in this area to my future employer."

Gen Z's interest in diversity spans race, gender, sexual orientation, and different gender expressions, and they expect companies to recruit a workforce that represents a truly inclusive culture where people of all kinds of backgrounds can thrive. Many young women I interviewed told me they study the composition of a company leadership team to gauge the prospect of career opportunities for themselves. They also will not hesitate to ask if a prospective employer pays men and women equally if they perform the same roles.

Companies should also give Gen Zers the opportunity to make a personal impact. In my research, 51 percent of Gen Z said volunteer programs are an important factor when choosing an employer (see Figure 6.1). Companies need to create opportunities throughout the year, either through organized campaigns or by giving employees time to focus on a cause of their choice. For example, Salesforce employees are eligible to take up to 56 hours of paid volunteer time off (VTO) per year to support their communities, and the company will match nonprofit donations up to $5,000 per year.[103]

Partially a response to the growing demand from Millennial workers, who viewed social good as an important feature of the workplace, the last decade has witnessed a significant increase in companies that offer personal time off to volunteer. By one estimate, 25 percent of companies did so in 2018, compared to 15 percent in 2009.[104]

In addition to improved employee engagement, studies show that "volunteering helps cultivate the soft skills that are increasingly important for knowledge workers: collaboration, empathy, adaptability, leadership, and public speaking."[105]

But They Are Also Realistic . . .

One should not conflate GenZ's idealism with naivete. The contrary is true.

Gen Zers have clear expectations for their financial future and personal growth. Having been raised by the pragmatic Gen Xers, their starting point in life was already placing them on the path of being realistic and practical. They want companies to pay them well and promote them quickly. "Gen Z is very financially motivated and have very high compensation expectations for an entry level," said Christine Waddick of Sun Life Canada.

List with Clever, an online real estate service, surveyed undergraduate students in 2019 about their expectations for compensation. The company found that students on average expect to make roughly $58,000 one year into their careers, compared to the national median salary of $47,000 for people with a bachelor's degree. They also prioritize employee benefits differently from Millennials: "They rank tangible, money-based incentives—like competitive salaries and excellent insurance plans—above a fun work environment, flex time, and unlimited PTO. In fact, Gen Zers say earning more money throughout their careers is the number-one reason why they want to earn a college degree."[106]

In addition to monetary compensation, Gen Z wants to rise quickly in the workplace. Eighty three percent of Gen Zers who participated in my research said having opportunities for promotion is an important consideration when choosing an employer, a figure that was slightly higher than Millennials (79 percent) and Gen X (74 percent) (see Figure 6.1). "It's important to me to have opportunities to move up the ladder in a company," Jacob said. "If I see a clear path for me to work hard and have that hard work translate into other positions or other opportunities, I will consider it as an attractive proposition."

To achieve their career goals, Gen Zers know they need help. Sixty eight percent of my research participants said access to mentors and training is a crucial factor in picking an employer (see Figure 6.1). Dylan said, "Mentoring and being able to learn from those who have been there before me and have role models to look up to, is critical." And according to many human resources executives I interviewed, the new generation of employees not only seeks on-the-job training and mentoring, but also asks companies to invest in their own personal development and personal growth in the form of company contributions to language classes or public speaking training and the like.

With the right programs, employers can help Gen Zers identify strengths and passions (while preserving a high level of engagement with the company) and ultimately retain them. Gen Z is highly motivated and ready to work hard to advance their careers. They know that training and professional and personal growth opportunities are critical to success. Therefore, they will prioritize companies that can best appeal to their natural desire to learn and grow. As they enter a world that is defined by the four generations that came before them, employers will be faced with a new challenge—making Gen Z feel at home.

Chapter 6: The 360 View

Gen Z brings a set of expectations and seemingly contradictory characteristics to the workplace. Business leaders will have to understand these traits and adjust key processes and practices to successfully attract, recruit, train, and retain this new generation of employees.

Attract

- Employer branding has never been so crucial, and while it may sound obvious, research shows that there is major room for improvement in the way companies communicate their brand to potential recruits. Gen Zers want to know *why* they should join you. Your ability to clearly communicate the unique value proposition of your company *and* your industry can make or break their interest.
- Ensure that all your digital touchpoints—company website, social media channels, and review sites—convey your employer brand in a consistent manner. Be careful, though, and do not oversell yourself. Gen Z has a developed B.S. meter and they can easily spot inauthenticity. Being authentic could save you all the selling. Being inauthentic may cost you more than just money.
- Gen Zers prefer companies with clear values and purpose and expect that your higher purpose is reflected in your employee value proposition. Is volunteer-time-off part of what you offer? Do you

support a cause that they care about? And if you do, what do you have to show for it?

Recruit

- A smooth, technology-driven process is a must when hiring Gen Zers. Interview scheduling tools, video résumés, video interviews, and text messages are just a few of the features that Gen Zers desire and leading companies already use as part of the recruiting process. But watch out and don't overdo it. Gen Z will view a fully automated process as a major turnoff. Make sure to balance automation with personal contact.
- Speed is of the essence when recruiting Gen Z. They will give up on you if they have not heard back from you promptly during the recruiting process. This kind of leverage may be weakened in a post-pandemic environment but it will not go away. "Gen Z will be Gen Z" when recruiting is back in full swing again.

Onboard

- Gen Z is entering the world of work during one of the most transformative periods in the history of business, when organizational complexity and constant change are an integral part of the workplace. Therefore, onboarding days, in addition to the traditional introduction to the company's vision, mission, and internal procedures, should focus on the *context* of their work (the "why"), the organization's ways of working, the interdependencies between functions, and some good tips on how to navigate these complexities.

Train and Develop

- Gen Z has a strong preference for working independently. Their entrepreneurial spirit, if channeled well, can deliver great value to any organization. They are willing to work hard, take on extra roles, and go the extra mile, but they need and expect close guidance and frequent feedback to thrive.

- Training and developing Gen Zers requires more coaching, less managing. Remember, Gen Z may not be fully prepared for a 21st-century workplace where soft skills are as important as technical skills. These skills can only be coached, not taught. Are your managers, at all levels, ready to coach?
- Gen Z has a strong preference for visual communication. They are likely to comprehend a five-minute video better than a one-page memo, and they rather consume new knowledge in small chunks that they can access on the go. Take that into account when planning training.
- Give Gen Zers opportunities to leverage their digital skills. Reverse or reciprocal mentoring will go a long way, giving them an opportunity to shine and make an impact.

Retain

- Gen Z's list of expectations from the workplace is long; they value employer benefits, above market compensation, hyper-flexibility, opportunities to advance and more. You can always refer to Figure 6.1 for the full list. In addition, Gen Z values community and a sense of belonging, which requires leaders who can show that they truly care about their subordinates' well-being and long-term development as well as recognize their contribution.
- "Change is the only constant" is a Gen Z mantra. As we saw in Part I of this book, experiencing major life-defining events during their formative years made them highly adaptive to change. We all know how hard it is to implement change in an organization, so coaching Gen Z employees to act as change champions or play an important role in change programs could be a win-win for both business leaders and Gen Z employees.

My biggest dream is to be a CEO of a company and use my wealth and power to change the world.

Dreamer: Abigail, 19, New York

Artist: Bea Vaquero, 36, Melbourne, Australia

CHAPTER 7

A Multigenerational Workforce

THE HOLIDAY DINNER has long been a staple of American culture. Every Thanksgiving and Christmas, family members from across the country reunite, share turkey and eggnog, and spend quality time with each other as the old year slips into the new one. At least that's the popular narrative. The reality is that the festive setting is sometimes a breeding ground for tension and pure dysfunction. Skeletons emerge from the closet, grudges resurface, resentment and disappointment boil over, and then someone brings up politics.

People seem to tolerate the ritual gatherings perhaps because they know the holidays only last a few days. But now imagine a much bigger group of interconnected people essentially having a holiday dinner over and over every day for most of the year. And instead of the usual nuclear family spats, you have five generations of people simultaneously jostling for acceptance and the moral high ground. That's exactly the scenario that companies are about to face.

As Gen Z enters the workforce, for the first time in history, five generations of employees will be working together under one roof, at least for a short time (see Figure 7.1). Though the last of the Silent Generation is expected to exit the workforce in the next year or so, and Baby Boomers are leaving the workforce in droves, not everyone retires at age 65. According to the Pew Research Center, in 2018 roughly 30 percent of Boomers aged 65 to 72 were still working or looking for work,[107] creating a labor phenomenon that we have not seen before.

Figure 7.1. Five Generations in the Workforce

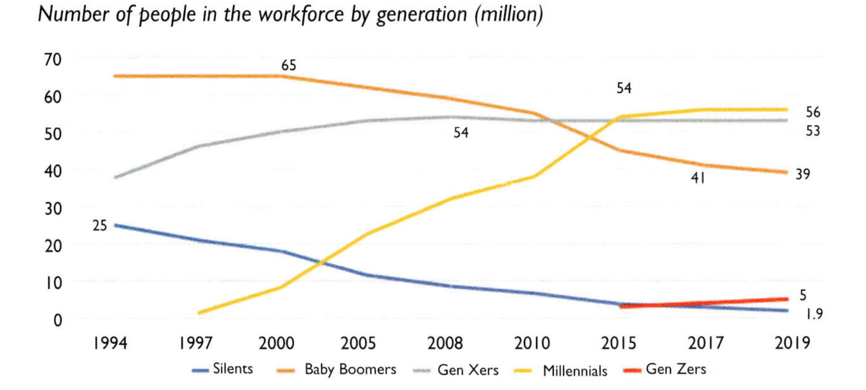

Source: Data for 1992-2017 courtesy of Pew Research Center. 2018-2019 data: U.S. Bureau of Labor Statistics

In short, the U.S. workforce is getting older. The U.S. Bureau of Labor Statistics estimates that employees age 55 and older will account for 25 percent of workers by 2028, compared to 12.5 percent in 1998.[108] Gen Z, whose oldest members recently celebrated their 23rd birthday, will join a workforce with almost fifty-year gap between the oldest and the youngest employee: Silent Generation members (mid-70s+), Baby Boomers (mid-50s to mid-70s), Gen Xers (early 40s to mid-50s), and Millennials (mid-20s to early 40s).

Each generation has its own views about what makes a good employee, how work should get done, and what they can expect from the workplace. The highly disciplined and conservative members of the Silent Generation, who grew up during the Great Depression, value service, sacrifice, prudence, and loyalty to work. "This generation is known for their appreciation of hierarchy and boundaries . . . they can be resistant to change, which could can make it difficult for them to adapt to the newer cohorts in their workplace."[109] In 2019, only 1.9 million members of this generation were still in the workforce.[110] Most of them will likely retire soon.

Baby Boomers, the first generation to be associated with "career first," are synonymous with hard work, competition, and long workdays. Careers have provided many Boomers with a source of fulfillment and a sense of identity. Growing up during the 1960s and 1970s amid the civil rights movement and opposition to the Vietnam War, Boomers are comfortable with challenging the establishment and believe they can drive change. They are both idealistic and optimistic. Their careers were launched and flourished at a time when corporate America was defined by organizational hierarchies, the corner office, rigid processes, and overall formal corporate culture. That made it difficult for them to come to terms with the changes that were brought by the following generations, especially Millennials, who value flatter organization structures, collaboration, work-life balance, and an informal work culture. Boomers are still holding many leadership positions, but many are entering the last leg of their careers.

Generation X represents a departure from the die-hard attitude of the Boomers. For this pragmatic generation, a job is just a job. They work to live and are results-oriented. In contrast with the idealism and optimism of the Boomers, they are pessimistic and somewhat cynical. "Having grown up as the 'latch key' children, they are independent, resourceful, and self-sufficient. They are the first generation to grow up with computers and technology, so they adapt more easily to technological change. They value freedom, responsibility and work-life balance and espouse a work hard/play hard mentality."[111] Gen Xers are likely to hold middle to senior positions. They are raising families and prioritize their children's education.

According to the Pew Research Center, Millennials became the largest generation in the workforce in 2016.[112] This generation had previously delayed homeownership, marriage, and starting families but are now focusing on these priorities. Having grown up with technology, Millennials believe companies should not limit work to 9-5 inside a physical office. This generation launched the hyper-flexibility trend. They are ambitious, entrepreneurial, and highly collaborative, and they value community service. Their expectations for a fun and collaborative work environment paved the way to office space redesigns. Millennials wanted everything on their own terms but were not so inclined to offer their loyalty in return. They are constantly searching for the next opportunity and, generally speaking, prefer experiences over material goods. Companies have struggled to fully understand this generation, often mistaking their need for flexibility and their demand for work-life balance with a sense of entitlement.

Gen Z is entering this multigenerational melting pot with its own set of values and expectations. In addition, they have a genuine concern about the way they are perceived by older generations and the potential impact it could have on their work experience. In my research, Gen Zers noted relationships with older generations as one of the top 10 challenges they face. They believe that older generations don't think much of their character or abilities. Brandon, who had an opportunity to work in several places during his college years before landing a job with his current nonprofit employer, told me: "Attitudes toward young people tend to vary by organization, but there is an overall negative connotation with us. They [older colleagues] tend to think that we are a little soft . . . or that we can't handle criticism and that we rely too much on technology. . . . They just don't like what they don't understand."

Unfortunately, his and other Gen Zers' concerns are not misplaced. According to a national survey of workplace managers, "more than a third believe that managing Gen Z employees will be more difficult than managing previous generations." Managers mostly anticipate communication and training-related challenges.[113] My own research suggests that older generations question the loyalty of Gen Z. They also suspect that Gen Z's constant connectivity and short attention span might distract them and thus negatively impact the quality of their work.

Generational feuding, like those tense holiday dinners, is nothing new. Older people may see their younger counterparts as entitled, soft, and ungrateful. Younger people may think older generations are out of touch and inflexible. Companies therefore should carefully craft strategies to avoid the workplace equivalent of a dysfunctional holiday dinner and integrate employees from multiple generations into a cohesive, harmonious workforce. The process starts by understanding differences—actual and perceived.

Different Values, Different Working Styles, and Unconscious Biases

Workplace diversity, whether in gender, race, or age, can serve companies well by allowing them to tap into a variety of perspectives, experiences, and expertise to solve problems and generate ideas. A 2018 study by Randstad revealed that over 85 percent of the people they surveyed "preferred to work in multigenerational teams and that they come up with innovative ideas and solutions thanks to being part of age-diverse teams." A similar number believed that "collaboration between generations is mutually beneficial at their companies."[114]

However, conflict can arise from generational differences in values and working styles as well as from unconscious bias and stereotyping.

For example, younger generations are more inclined to value work-life balance than are older workers, leading to the well-known stereotypes like "Millennials are entitled" or "Gen Zers are lazy."

Angel Hu, an organizational psychologist based in New York City, told me, "It is very hard for Boomers to accept this [generational] shift; they feel that they had to do things in certain ways, that they worked very hard, and that now others should follow and earn their dues." For their part, younger employees view their high student loan debt as an economic disadvantage unique to their generation. They believe that they "did not have it as good" as previous generations.

According to Hu, Gen Zers' attitudes toward gender fluidity and activism are additional potential areas of conflict with older workers. "Freedom of expression is extremely important to Gen Z," she said. "It could manifest in the way they define themselves, their use of pronouns, or their sartorial choices, which may be hard for older employees who grew up in a more conservative era to relate to or accept." Gen Z's tendency to integrate work with personal politics could clash with older generations who had set strict boundaries between their personal and professional lives. Hu noted:

> Younger generations want to show up at work with their "whole-self". . . a.k.a "authenticity." You don't hear Baby Boomers talk about authenticity [in the workplace]. For them, work is work. And while for Gen Z, expecting that a company will have a purpose or act on its diversity and inclusion agenda is natural and human, older generations might view it as a political statement or as a political act, and politics for them has no place at the workplace.

Brandon has a similar view: "My age group is very self-expressive. We're open to talking about things like our feelings and everything, and they [older employees] might perceive that as a weakness."

But Dennis Shuler, an executive chairman of Kinetic Consulting in North America, former chief human resources officer at Walt Disney, Kellogg, Scripps Networks Interactive, and NXP Semiconductors, and a retired officer of Procter & Gamble, thinks Gen Z's demand for authenticity will benefit companies. He told me: "In the past, employees took everything they were told as a gospel, and Gen Z is set to question everything. They want the detail behind any claim a company makes, which can be challenging to some. But ultimately, Gen Z's insistence on truth, transparency, and authenticity will raise the overall quality of what companies are doing. The quality of the conversation, the quality of the feedback, and the quality of the management—it has the potential to raise the standards for the rest of the organization if it is embraced."

Clashing work styles could be an additional source of friction. Baby Boomers and Gen Xers grew up in a more hierarchal environment where managers were "telling" and "directing." By contrast, Millennials prefer a more participative style. One interesting challenge for employers to watch is how Gen Z will interact with Millennials, who are likely to be their bosses. Millennials now hold approximately a third of the U.S. workforce's management positions,[115] and their penchant for collaboration might clash with the individualistic leanings of Gen Zers.

Left unchecked, generational conflict could lead to resentment, unconscious bias, and age-based stereotyping. These are the "silent killers of engagement, collaboration, and productivity," according to a study by AchieveGlobal, a leadership development firm. In general, the study found that "younger employees were more likely to think they are 'more efficient in multitasking and more creative' than older workers."[116] For their part, "older employees were more likely to think that they 'have a stronger work ethic' than younger workers and that younger employees 'demand more recognition.'"[117] Perhaps the study's most unsettling finding was that employees in positions of power were more susceptible to the influence of age stereotypes.

Samantha experienced that firsthand when she started working. At her retail store, she reports to a store manager who is in her late 20s, who reports to a district manager who is in his 50s. On her first day, she was welcomed by the store manager, who happened to share with her that during the interview process the district manager had some reservations about her potential to succeed because "she is too young." Samantha found that disturbing and disheartening, yet it motivated her to prove him wrong.

Integrating Four Generations

Experts say companies should embrace four strategies to increase understanding and acceptance among workers of different generations, reduce tension, and in turn protect productivity. The strategies are: providing training, creating mixed teams, providing reciprocal mentoring, and offering differentiated benefits.

First is **training**. Dennis Shuler believes that a progressive company should offer training to help people understand generational differences: "These sessions can examine the events and experiences that shaped each generation's worldview, but even more important, these training sessions should highlight commonalities." Each generation, according to Shuler, has similar hopes and dreams related to their careers. Everyone wants to work in a company where they can be themselves, where there is a sense of purpose to what they do, where they contribute their full potential, where they work for managers who are interested in them as "individuals," not as "workers," and where they get good feedback. "Those truths are universal, whether you grew up in the 1970s or if you are in your twenties," he said. "Emphasizing these commonalities could help bring people together."

The second strategy is **creating mixed teams**. Angel Hu referred to a psychological phenomenon called the "mere exposure effect," in which "encountering a stimulus repeatedly somehow makes one like it more. The stimulus could be a melody on a radio or a face of a person you pass by every day—somehow these stimuli tend to grow on you."[118] Therefore, companies should get employees from across generations familiar with each other by exposing them to each other's ideas and working styles in a structured way. Specifically, Hu suggests creating cross-generational groups to work on a project not directly related to their daily work. They would need to collaborate with each other to accomplish a shared goal. Such groups could help alleviate anxiety and tension that comes from generational differences. The projects could also help employees recognize everyone's skills and strengths and see that workers, young and old, can contribute and learn from each other.

The third strategy is **reciprocal mentoring**. A trend that started with Millennials as "reverse mentoring" was intended to leverage Millennials' digital savviness so they could educate older employees about digital technologies and social media. Reverse mentoring has morphed into reciprocal mentoring, in which an older employee mentors a young employee and vice versa. Since almost 70 percent of Gen Zers place a high value on personal development and mentoring (see Figure 6.1), reciprocal mentoring potentially offers companies an excellent strategy not only to attract young talent but also to bridge the gap with older generations.

The fourth strategy is **differentiated benefits** that are driven by employees' life stages. "Avoid one-size-fits-all," said Shuler. "What may be appealing to a Baby Boomer, like pension or health care, may not be as appealing to a younger employee, who may believe that they will have to work longer than their parents and might be more interested in clearing their student loan debt." Indeed, 60 percent of Gen Zers said that tuition reimbursement will be highly desirable if offered by an employer. Companies like Bank of America, Starbucks, and Home Depot are among a list of companies leading the way with this type of employment benefit.[119]

Stan Silverman, dean, and professor emeritus of social sciences at the University of Akron, told me that differentiated benefits must be managed carefully to not end up with negative effects. For example, flexible work hours, when given only to a select group of employees, could end up hurting them. Most notably, women felt that working flexible hours for family reasons had negatively affected their career progression. On the other hand, when flextime is offered across the board, employees have the opportunity to define what flexibility means to them, and the need for flexibility is de-stigmatized. "Every group has a need for flexibility for different reasons. . . . You have the young mother with small children who wants to come in late after taking her children to school, or the young dad who wants to be at home before his kids go to bed, but also the older employee who may need to care for an older parent and need to be able to take time off when needed."

So, What Does It Mean for Leadership?

Integrating and managing a multigenerational workforce cannot be viewed as simply another exercise in managing workplace diversity. Because Gen Z is arriving at a time of rapid technological disruption and societal changes, leaders must not only transform their organizations but also rethink their leadership styles in order to accommodate Gen Z's workplace expectations.

Most senior business leaders today are Gen Xers or Baby Boomers who grew up with a business leadership style that was top-down, direct, and controlling. "A few generations ago," said Dennis Shuler, "people had a mental picture of business leaders that was typically 'the tall white male with a booming voice' whose acts were described in military terms such as 'he is in charge' . . . "he leads from the front."" If language is a telling sign of an era, one only needs to think back to some of the prominent executives who had nicknames like "Neutron Jack" (Jack Welch), "Chainsaw Al" (Al Dunlap), and "Irv the Liquidator" (Irwin Jacobs).

In the post–World War II era, such a style helped establish the foundation for structures and processes critical for speed and scale. But those days are coming to an end because the nature of work itself has changed, because our culture has evolved to recognize the deficiencies of this style, and because a new generation of employees, starting with the Millennials, have different perspectives and values and want to be part of a more democratized workforce.

As Angel Hu sees it, today's leaders need to adopt a style that is more lateral, shared, and dynamic. They have to accept feedback from all sources and exercise compassion and empathy. These leaders will have to understand the value of emotional intelligence, diversity and inclusion, and people-related innovation. And according to Shuler, "Leaders today should focus on creating an environment that encourages people to reach their full potential, offer direction and purpose, build followership, meet people where they are, and connect people to the broader mission of the company so that they feel that they are part of something that is greater than themselves."

Gen Zers are seeking this type of leadership. Seventy percent of my research participants said that having access to inspiring leaders is an important factor when considering an employer. Wendy told me that her manager made all the difference for her: "A good leader is someone who can give constructive feedback and helps [my development]. My manager has a great attitude, he is very positive, he cares about what I am doing and how things are going for me. . . . He listens. . . . He is approachable . . . which helps me to be open with him and ask for help and learn."

Moreover, one thing that really separates Gen Z from previous generations is their impatience. If Gen Zers are unhappy with their jobs, they will leave a company much more rapidly than older workers, as we saw in Samantha's story. An exodus of young talent would be disastrous for companies operating in the whirlwind that is the present world economy. Therefore, companies must adapt accordingly if they want to attract and retain the best and the brightest young talent. Gen Z represents the future of work, and companies have to do all they can to embrace that future.

Chapter 7: The 360 View

- Gen Z is joining a multigenerational workforce that represents a gap of almost fifty years between the oldest and the youngest employees. Generational differences could lead to tension and conflict.
- Left unchecked, generational conflict could lead to resentment, unconscious bias, and age-based stereotyping that could negatively impact engagement, collaboration, and productivity in the workplace. Therefore to increase understanding and acceptance among workers and protect workplace productivity, companies should embrace four strategies:
  - **Training**. Provide opportunity for constructive learning by jointly examining the events and experiences that shaped each generation's worldview and find commonalities on which better working relationships can be established.
  - **Mixed teams**. Get employees from across generations familiar with each other by exposing them to each other's ideas and working styles in a structured way through work teams or through special projects that are not related to their day-to-day work.
  - **Reciprocal mentoring**. Pair a member of Gen Z with an older employee so they can learn from each other. Gen Zers bring their knowledge of youth culture and digital savviness, and they can benefit from an older colleague's experience on how to navigate the organization and their careers.
  - **Differentiated benefits.** Avoid a "one-size-fits-all" approach to benefits. What may be appealing to a Baby Boomer may not be as appealing to a younger employee. Identify what benefit programs suits each life stage and apply it accordingly.
- To successfully integrate Gen Z into a multigenerational workforce, managers and executives will have to adopt a more lateral, shared, and dynamic leadership style that encourages people to reach their full potential and connect them to the broader mission of the company.

My Biggest Dream...

To be a Yogi.

Michelle, 20, Hawaii

Become a FedEx pilot who travels the world while being paid for it.

Will, 20, Tennessee

Finish college in 4 years and pass the CPA exams on the first try.

Daniel, 17, California

To earn an advanced degree in Electrical Engineering and work for a leading global company.

Justin, 17, Virginia

Become a doctor and save people's lives.

Caroline, 18, Massachusetts

My dream is to work hard and find my place in the world.

Dreamer: Andrew, 19, Massachusetts

Artist: Alfonso Cirillo aka Fonzy Nils, 30, Milan, Italy

PART III

Commerce

CHAPTER 8
A Rising (Purchasing) Power

- A funeral for Mr. Peanut.
- Bill Murray reliving the 1993 movie *Groundhog Day* for Jeep.
- Josh Jacobs offers advice to his younger self while driving a new Kia model.
- Lil Nas X and actor Sam Elliott battle for a bag of Doritos.
- Lilly Singh and Busy Philipps on behalf of Olay take a trip into outer space with a hashtag #makespaceforwomen.
- Real people come together to deliver a message "Whatever you rock, there is a Facebook group for you."

THESE ARE JUST a few examples of the 2020 Super Bowl commercials. Besides being indicators of cultural and advertising trends, Super Bowl commercials offer a window into the priorities of the companies behind the ads. This particular season it was clear that corporate America was eyeing the next generation of consumers. Using themes such as nostalgia (Jeep), gender equality (Olay), community (Facebook), and purpose (Kia) and featuring well-known Gen Zers like TikTok star Charli D'Amelio and singer Lil Nas X, brands signaled the importance of the rising Gen Z consumer. And rightly so! Gen Z is set to shake up the world of commerce in a very big way, and consumer brands better be prepared.

The importance of Gen Z to the consumer market stems not only from the sheer size of their cohort (78 million people), which will translate over time into a significant purchasing power, but also from their attitudes toward earning, saving, and spending, which will force brands to rethink how they go to market and how they engage them. Combined data from the U.S. Bureau of Labor Statistics and my own research suggest that in 2019 Gen Zers had a direct purchasing power of nearly $280 billion.[120] The majority of this amount was held by those who are 16 years old and up, who gained it through full-time or part-time employment, summer jobs, side hustles, or support from their parents. The younger Gen Zers typically rely on parental allowances or odd jobs like babysitting or dog walking.

But Gen Z's purchasing power goes well beyond the money they earn or receive. According to research by the National Retail Federation (NRF), "nearly 9 in 10 parents say their children influence 36 percent of the purchases they made for the household and 48 percent of the purchases they make for the kids themselves."[121] This is not surprising, considering the strong bond between Gen X parents and their Gen Z kids. While the parents get involved in every aspect of their kids' lives, they also involve the kids in key decisions related to the running of the household. From buying a car to picking a dining-out location, Gen Z influence reaches deep.

Parents I interviewed repeatedly emphasized the importance of involving their kids in purchasing decisions. Many of them saw it as an opportunity to teach their kids the value of money and to let them wrestle with the tradeoffs that come with choosing one product over another and with the accountability for their decision once they made a choice. "My kids influence 70 percent of our household purchases," said Maureen, a San Francisco–based mother of two Gen Z kids, ages eleven and eight. "My daughter started to search products online when she was nine. . . . She knows where to look for products and is extremely cost-conscious, searching for [the] best prices on multiple sites." When I asked her daughter, Clare, how she determines if a cheap product is of good quality, she answered without hesitation, "I read the reviews and see what other people have to say."

Gen Zers, across all ages, are extremely savvy and empowered consumers who make purchasing decisions every day: paying for music and film downloads, shopping online or in stores, or signing up for a new subscription. Combined with their broader influence on household expenditures, Gen Z is emerging as an attractive segment for brands and service providers alike. To truly evaluate their potential, one must first understand how they think about money, savings, and spending.

Financial Security—A Core Value

Attitudes toward money and approaches to personal finances have always been shaped by the economic and social context that each generation has experienced. Millennials, for example, found themselves with high student loan debt and difficulties finding suitable jobs as young adults. They responded with a more risk-averse approach to their finances, delaying or questioning the need for homeownership, and avoiding debt and investments in equity. A study by BlackRock, the investment management firm, suggests that Millennials keep 65 percent of their assets in cash, compared to the national average of 58 percent, because they fear a catastrophic market event.[122]

Similarly, Gen Z's approach to money is influenced by their experiences. Gen Zers have been greatly affected by the 2008 recession—seeing their parents dealing with the loss of a job or a home or with the anxiety that this might happen—as well as by watching their Millennial siblings and friends dealing with the consequences of student loan debt. In addition, the COVID-19 pandemic has added another layer of influence. Of the Gen Zers ages 18–22 that I polled during the pandemic, 42 percent said that the pandemic has influenced their family finances, while 28 percent said it has had a direct impact on their job situation, in the form of layoffs, furloughs, or reduced hours. As a result, Gen Zers have evolved into a highly aware, highly motivated group of young people who are determined to do better and do whatever they can to learn from the mistakes of others and secure their financial future as early as possible.

Gen Zers who participated in my research ranked financial security among the top things they value in life, second only to family. Moreover, when asked to share their biggest dream, roughly one in five listed financial security, financial freedom, and being able to support a family in the future as their biggest aspirations. Statements in the spirit of "being financially stable and independent without sacrificing my freedom or my sense of adventure" or "to be financially secure and be able to support my family and help other people in need" were common.

As a result, Gen Zers have an inclination toward savings. Nearly half of those who participated in my research said they save a quarter or more of the money they earn or receive from their parents. When asked what they would do if they were given a windfall of $1,000, 53 percent said they would save the money. Sarah, who worked throughout her high school years as a cashier of a flower nursery, told me: "I don't really spend much. Once I pay my car insurance and some basic things, I save the rest. I have some money in a money market account that earns some good interest. For me, saving money is a huge thing. I don't want to live paycheck to paycheck."

Save Early, Save Often

While the older Gen Zer's conservative approach to money is driven by their childhood experience of adverse economic conditions, the younger Gen Zers are evolving into big savers because of the increased exposure to financial information online and the rise of technological tools that allow them to experience money in a very different way from previous generations.

One example of these tools is a payment card called *gohenry,* which was created by a group of parents who shared similar concerns about teaching children how to manage money in a digital world. Dean Brauer, one of the founders, shared with me how it all started: "The founders, based in the United Kingdom, were out watching their kids play football and having a conversation about how their kids were using their credit cards to make purchases on iTunes or Amazon. They were concerned about the lack of oversight of their kids' spending as well as over the fact that not dealing with 'real money' impacts how one values it." The conversation also had a nostalgic tone to it. None of the kids, when given money, would do what the parents used to do—run to the corner store to buy candy. Instead, they ended up somewhere online, buying music, shopping, and streaming video games. The parents, who later became business partners, agreed that raising kids in a cashless society is a challenge. As Brauer said, "Gen Z will be the first cashless generation, so if money is not something they can touch, they will need the right tools to help them learn about the value of money and gain confidence in managing it." Finding out that children and teens are the segment least served by traditional banks (in the United States, debit cards are issued only to those who are at least 13 years old), the trio went on to form *gohenry*, a company that is on a mission to help millions of kids to be good with money.

Financial institutions' limited offerings for younger demographics were also the key trigger for the creation of Rebellion, a Spanish financial tech startup that offers a fully operational bank account for 14- to 24-year-olds. The company's chief operating officer, Gin Gindre, told me that he was particularly struck by the "mismatch between the many consumer services that are available to or specifically targeted at Gen Z, such as Netflix, Amazon, or Spotify, and the few payment solutions that were designed to address the needs of a digitally driven generation. Instead, most [kids] used their parents' cards to pay for the services."

According to Brauer, who is now spearheading the expansion of *gohenry* in the United States, "In places where there is a culture of giving kids allowances, parents increasingly need tools to help them pass on the values that they feel are important as well as give kids freedom and independence to start managing the money themselves." He noted that approximately 70 percent of parents in the United States give their children regular allowances.

Solutions like the *gohenry* app allow kids as young as six to use a card that is paired with an app that comes with parental controls and budgeting tools designed specifically for kids and teens. Parents can add money to the app, set an automatic weekly allowance, add tasks with assigned monetary values for the kids to earn, set spending limits, and decide where the card can be used. Most important, the parents can feel confident about giving the kids some freedom to manage their own money. For their part, the kids experience the fundamentals of money management: earning, spending, saving, and giving (donating) money. According to Brauer, "Most of the available research indicates that people form their attitudes and habits toward money at age six or seven . . . and parents play the biggest role in shaping those attitudes. Therefore, it's important for kids to start young and for parents to have a tool to help pass on positive money management behaviors."

Considering Gen Z's natural inclination toward technology and digital tools, these payment solutions can be very beneficial. Based on *gohenry*'s experience, when kids are given cash, they want to spend it immediately, but when they are given digital tools, they develop a sense of ownership and an awareness of what comes in and goes out and they go from being spenders to being savers. "Eighty-six percent of the parents who participate in the *gohenry* community believe that their kids became better at managing money because of the app and card. When you give kids an opportunity to learn for themselves, great things happen," Brauer said.

Planning Ahead: The Future Starts Now

One would think that the savings objectives for people as young as Gen Zers would be to buy the latest sneakers or the newest piece of electronics. And while that is true to an extent, the majority of Gen Zers seem to be future-oriented and pragmatic in their thinking about money. When asked what they are saving for, a quarter of my research participants said that they save for short-term or ongoing expenditures, such as entertainment, going out, clothing, car insurance, bill payments, or other necessities. Thirty percent said that first and foremost, they feel the need to build an emergency fund and save for a rainy day. "I save money because I want to be prepared and have a backup for anything that comes up, [any] unforeseen circumstances," wrote one of the participants. Saving is a sensible course of action at a time when the Federal Reserve data shows that 40 percent of American adults would have difficulty covering $400 of unexpected expenses.[123] The rest of the participants were split between saving for their education and saving for large purchases like a car or a house.

College is a top financial concern for Gen Zers who said that they save either to pay their tuition or just to ensure that they can cover some of their expenses while in school. Despite the bad reputation student loans have received, mostly due to the large debt carried by Millennials, over half of my research participants said they plan to take out a student loan or use a combination of a loan and family support. Max, a 16-year-old who lives in Colorado, told me he does plan to take out a loan: "My parents can pay for my college, but I would feel guilty if they did. I plan to work this summer and put half of the money toward college." Other Gen Zers are planning to work throughout their time in college to supplement family support or to fully pay for their college years.

Gen Z's willingness to take financial responsibility is also showing in credit activity data. Matthew Komos, vice president of financial services research and consulting at TransUnion, a credit reporting agency, told me, "Gen Z is increasingly active in the credit market and is driving growth across different credit products. Naturally, they are active in student loans, but we also see an increased activity in credit cards, auto loans, and mortgages." In the second half of 2019, the agency reported that 25 percent of Gen Z consumers had a balance-carrying credit card, up 40 percent from 2018.[124] According to Komos, delinquency rates among Gen Zers are low, indicating their sensible approach to credit and their sense of responsibility.

While mortgage applications by Gen Zers still represent a small percentage of the total market, it is the fastest-growing credit category, according to the TransUnion report, indicating Gen Z's inclination for planning ahead and their interest in homeownership—the embodiment of the American Dream. Compared to Millennials, who delayed homeownership, Gen Zers are eager to have a place to call their own, and they have a positive outlook on homeownership. When asked if they want to own a home in the future, 87 percent responded positively, compared to 63 percent of Millennials. Gen Zers view homeownership as a fundamental building block of wealth creation and financial security, and only 10 percent view it as a financial burden, compared to 19 percent of Millennials (see Figure 8.1).

Gen Zers not only have positive views about homeownership but also have concrete plans for it. According to a report by Bank of America, "59 percent of prospective homebuyers at the ages 18-23 are planning to buy a home in the next five years, meaning they would own a home before the age of 30. While certainly aspirational, this isn't just a pipe dream for Gen Z; more than half have already started saving, showing their commitment to this goal, and 71 percent say they know what they want in a home."[125]

Figure 8.1. Homeownership—Millennials vs. Gen Z

Q: Do you agree with the following statements?

Percentage of respondents who agreed with the statement

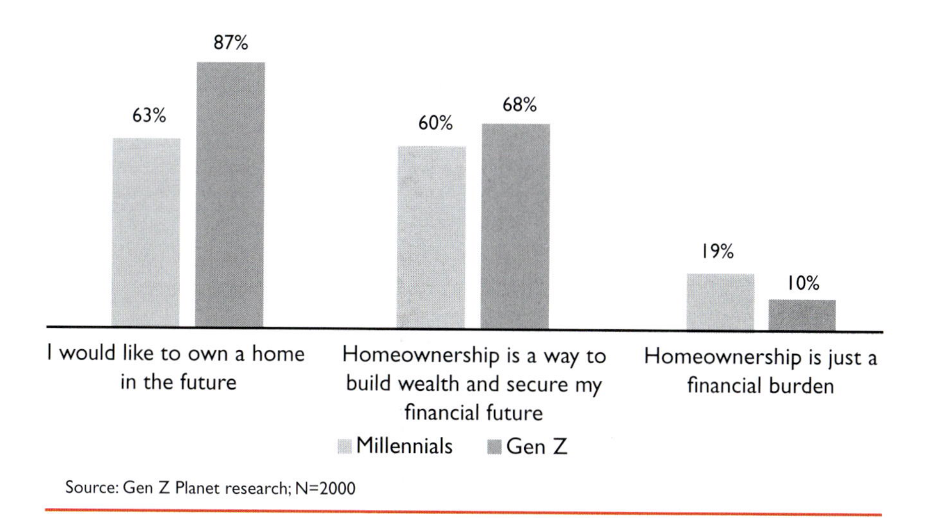

Source: Gen Z Planet research; N=2000

In an interview, J. Allen Seelenbinder, a senior vice president and division executive at the Mid America Consumer Lending Division of Bank of America, identified three reasons why Gen Z is viewing homeownership in a more positive light.

"First is the economic context," he said. "Gen Z has in their favor historic low interest rates and a favorable affordability index [a composite measure that considers supply and demand curves, interest rates, and access to credit] as well as a steady amount of appreciation in home value. By comparison, Millennials, who reached their household formation life stage around 2008, faced the reality of the housing crisis, recession, and declining home value which led them to delay homeownership." In addition, the student loan debt burden that Millennials carried was also a factor that delayed household formation. Seelenbinder believes, however, that things could be different for Gen Zers because of the way they approach college financing. Some Gen Zers start their education at a community college before transferring to a four-year college as a means of reducing cost, some take a gap year to work and save for college, and others plan to work during their college years to cover part of their expenses. In addition, the increase in the number of employers who offer tuition reimbursement could help some Gen Zers with their long-term financial planning.

Second, Gen Zers seem to be the beneficiaries of the lessons learned from the Great Recession. "The lending environment is different; there is greater commitment to distinct and affordable products for first-time home buyers. The options that are available today for this upcoming generation in the environment we're in are quite unprecedented, not to mention the support tools they come with," Seelenbinder said. Lending products today come with a host of educational programs, something that banks have been focused on in recent years. For example, the Better Money Habits program, a collaboration between Bank of America and the Khan Academy, was designed to offer online financial resources to young consumers. The program teaches everything from the principles of savings, home buying, down payments, and amortization to retirement savings. According to Seelenbinder, "Gen Zers want to learn themselves ... and the more comprehensive the resources are, the more they're going to gravitate toward them."

Consumer education is critical because consumers need to understand not only what their options are but also what risks are associated with home loans. "Part of responsible lending is giving the home buyer the education and the coaching to make a responsible decision," said Seelenbinder. In his experience, Gen Zers are already demonstrating that level of responsibility on multiple fronts. "They are more educated than the majority of individuals before them, and they are also more realistic about what they can spend."

Third is a collection of cultural forces that influence the views of Gen Z (or at least of some segments of the generation) on homeownership:

- **Demographics:** In many multicultural areas where families have been renting homes for a long time, Gen Zers are going to be the first generation to own a home, and there is a great sense of pride that comes with this ownership.
- **The changing job market:** Being employed by companies that allow employees to work remotely means that Gen Zers can buy homes in affordable locations while working for companies located in places that they would not be able to afford. This trend will most likely strengthen in a post-coronavirus world, when more companies will adopt remote working as a standard way of working.
- **The rise of Airbnb:** The cultural acceptance of renting out a room in one's home gives Gen Z the confidence that they can take on the responsibilities that come with ownership. Owning a home and renting a room to offset some of the cost is a common way of thinking among young borrowers.
- **Home improvement shows:** Gen Zers grew up watching home improvement TV programs such as *Property Brothers, Flip or Flop,* and *Fixer Upper* and saw how, with relatively little investment, they could create significant value and equity. "For Gen Zers, property is more than just a place to live," said Seelenbinder. "It's an investment, a lifestyle choice, and a platform for self-expression. The ability to personalize a home is an important factor. They have a vision. They are willing to buy properties that are not in perfect condition and make them their own."

Homeownership, however, is only one aspect of Gen Z's forward thinking and planning for their future. In addition, they are showing keen interest in investing and even in planning for retirement. In my conversation with Max, he said, "I started to look to invest in companies when I was fourteen years old. My math teacher once showed us what happens when you start investing early, and as soon as I am able, I plan to start a 401(k)."

Likewise, Jacob told me that he puts all the income he receives from his part-time job into a Roth IRA. "I totally save for retirement," he said.

Jennifer Barrett, chief education officer at Acorns, the micro-investment platform, is not surprised. "Gen Z awareness, if not their knowledge of investing, is higher than previous generations," she told me, attributing their interest in investing to their formative years. "Having seen the impact of the recession on the retirement accounts of their parents and grandparents and being exposed to the ongoing national debate about the cost of health care, Gen Zers are not counting on Social Security as much as previous generations did. They feel it is going to be on them to save money for retirement, and they start thinking about it early, which is impressive."

And if there is a gap between awareness, knowledge, and actual investment, companies like Acorns are stepping in to close it—one customer at a time. Acorns is on a mission "to look after the financial best interests of the up-and-coming, beginning with the empowering step of micro-investing."[126] By allowing users to invest their spare change, Acorns removes the biggest barrier that Americans, and particularly young people, have to investing, which is the perception that they don't have enough money to invest. Or as Barrett put it: "In reality, investing as little as five dollars at a time can go a long way for young people who have a long-term horizon."

Acorns "rounds up" the amount of money spent by its users on everyday purchases. These small roundups are transferred into the users' accounts and are invested in one of Acorns' five portfolios, giving young investors access to exchange traded funds (ETFs) and thousands of bonds and stocks, resulting in a diversified portfolio for each user. "We make portfolio recommendations based on users' responses to a series of questions that help us determine their risk appetite," said Barrett, adding that Gen Zers are showing a preference for a more aggressive risk profile investment than older customers. This is partially driven by the long-term horizon they have and by their eagerness to take part in the overall positive market performance of recent years.

As chief education officer, Barrett cannot emphasize enough the importance of financial literacy and education and the role that companies like Acorns play in improving it. "As a country we have not made great progress in introducing financial literacy curriculum into our high schools and colleges. From that standpoint, there is no reason to expect that Gen Zers will be more financially educated. Therefore, we do provide education, introduction to investing, savings, insurance as well as money basics on our website," she said.

Gen Z, according to Barrett, is going to be quite discerning about the apps they are going to use to grow their money: "In a highly competitive market, creating products that resonate with Gen Z means communicating in accessible, conversational language and delivering educational experiences that look more like the social media world rather than a textbook. They want to consume education in small digestible chunks that are more visual and fun."

There is no doubt that the competitive landscape for banking, savings, and investing has shifted significantly in the past decade. Traditional banks are competing with "challenger" banks. The traditional payment providers are competing with tech giants like Google, Apple, and Amazon Pay and with emerging platforms like Venmo and Zelle. Banks and investment firms are competing with a host of emerging investment apps like Robinhood and Acorns.

While technology plays a big role in this shift, it is Gen Z's digital savviness and adoption of these new tools that will accelerate their impact. And while many Gen Zers are using the large banks, their diversification into digital tools means that traditional banks are losing their traditional "one-stop shop" position, not to mention the full visibility they used to have of their customers' financials, which will make it harder for them to compete.

In most of the conversations I had with executives from both established and emerging financial firms, financial education was highlighted as one of the biggest opportunities in serving the next generation; so is the need to rethink at what age you start serving them. Banks have shied away in the past from serving young consumers who may not have much money to justify the cost of service. Yet, considering the competitive landscape, offering services to younger consumers may be the best pathway for long-term value creation.

Marcel van Oost, who founded several financial tech companies and is now advising others, has been monitoring the recent innovations and the way they are adopted by young users. In an interview he emphasized: "You can no longer ignore Gen Z. Kids, teens, and young adults—each segment is ripe with opportunities."

How Do They Spend It?

While Gen Z is more conservative about personal finances, that hardly means they will be tying up all of their earnings in houses and retirement accounts. Therefore, understanding where they spend their money is a good starting point to understanding who they are as consumers. When I asked my research participants to indicate where they spend most of their money, an interesting pattern emerged. For both younger and older Gen Zers, eating out was a top spending category, followed by clothing and footwear and entertainment (see Figure 8.2).

As one would expect, for older Gen Zers transportation (including car payments, car insurance, and maintenance), groceries, and utility bills tend to feature more often as top spending categories as some members of this generation already own cars and/or no longer live with their parents. For female participants, spending on beauty and cosmetics featured more often as one of their top three spending categories, placing it as a fourth category for young women.

Gen Z has already made a significant impact in these top categories.

Figure 8.2. Top Spending Categories

Q: Please pick the three categories on which you spend most of your money

Percentage of Gen Z respondents who picked a category as one of their top three

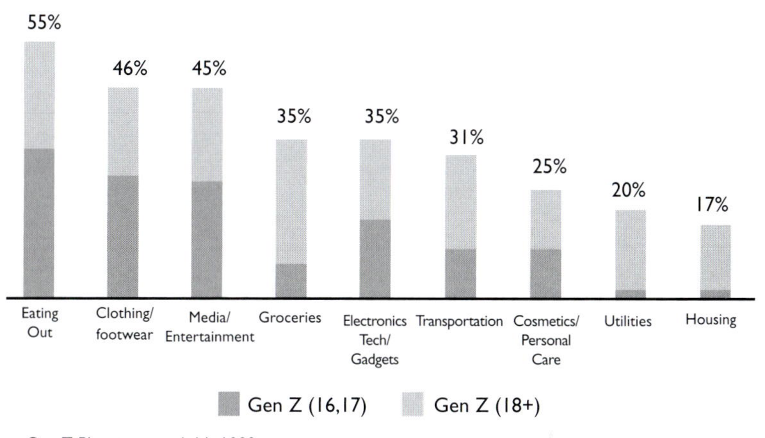

Source: Gen Z Planet research N=1000

In the food service industry they represented a quarter of the total traffic in 2018, according to the NPD Group, and they made almost an identical number of online food orders as Millennials did that same year—a staggering number considering that "only a portion of Gen Zs are old enough to order their own delivery."[127] On the fashion front, Gen Zers have been at the forefront of trends like re-commerce. They reenergized '90s fashion and gave a boost to brands like Fila and Champion as well as accelerated an already strong athletic footwear and clothing trend. In addition, as we saw in Part I of the book, Gen Z made a name for themselves as both users and producers of entertainment. Through their phones, they stream everything from YouTube videos to Netflix films, live-stream Twitch games, or create their own Instagram stories and TikTok videos. While they "Netflix and Chill," they also keep entertainment industry executives on their toes. Their viewing habits have led not only to further fragmentation of the streaming market but also to an increased demand for original content. The term "streaming wars" was not created for nothing.

There is no doubt, Gen Z is here and is ready to make its mark on the consumer market. As the competition over their wallets heats up, it will not be enough to simply know their basic demographics and spending patterns. To understand what makes Gen Z a unique consumer segment we have to dig into the "how" and "why" they are changing everything we know about commerce.

Chapter 8: The 360 View

- Gen Z is set to shake up the world of commerce in a big way. Their importance as consumers comes not only from their sheer size as a cohort of 78 million people but also from their growing purchasing power and their attitudes toward spending and saving, which set them apart from previous generations.
- Growing up during the Great Recession, watching the wealth inequality widening, and experiencing the economic impact of the COVID-19 pandemic, Gen Zers have developed a financially conservative attitude toward money. They are highly committed to secure their financial future, prioritizing savings and being cautious with spending. Being the true digital natives and having access to tools and applications that offer financial education and tracking of balances, they started savings and investing at an early age; some are even saving for retirement.
- Gen Zers are not only saving for a rainy day but also eyeing large purchases like cars and homes. They view homeownership favorably and are willing to compromise other areas of spending to save for their future. In recent years they emerged as active credit customers, and data shows that they act responsibly when it comes to meeting their financial obligations.
- While Gen Z is more conservative about personal finances, that hardly means they will be tying up all of their earnings in houses and retirement accounts. America is a shopping nation, after all, and Gen Z is no different. Eating out, clothing and footwear, and entertainment are the three biggest areas on which they spend their money. In these and other categories, Gen Zers bring a new set of expectations and behaviors—"The Gen Z way." It will require retailers and brands to fundamentally shift the way they think about, interact with, and build relationships with the next generation of consumers.

My dream is to own a home.

Dreamer: Brianna, 18, Michigan

Artist: Francisco Fonseca, 26, Porto, Portugal

CHAPTER 9

Gen Z Consumers—Accelerating Disruption

IN THE PAST decade, consumer-goods companies and retailers have experienced constant disruption on multiple fronts. Their traditional models that were built on frequent product introductions, mass production, mass advertising, and clearly defined media and distribution channels have been challenged by a host of trends. E-commerce sales have risen exponentially. Emerging direct-to-consumer brands, such as Warby Parker or Glossier, took a bite in the market share of established brands, demonstrating that they can do everything better, faster, and at a lower cost. New business models such as Rent the Runway and Dollar Shave Club have challenged old assumptions about how we consume products, and a host of digital technologies have transformed every part of the brand-to-store value chain. Add to that the impact of a global pandemic, and you get an orderly world turned upside down. A world in which declining sales, lost market share, low mall traffic, and store closures have become too common.

It would be easy to attribute all of these changes to technology, but that alone is not enough to explain the level of disruption. Driving these changes are the shifts in consumers' beliefs, values, and behaviors, *including* the use of technology. And it is *the* reason why Gen Z, with their distinct set of values and understanding of the power of technology, is set to accelerate the disruption.

Gen Z's values and points of view on social justice, equality, economic, and environmental issues have shaped their expectations from brands and their purchasing behaviors. So does the way they view and use technology. From researching topics of interest to making an investment, shopping the latest trend, or creating a movement, Gen Zers have demonstrated an uncanny ability to leverage technology to shake up brands and regulators. As they gain earning power and start making independent purchasing decisions, we will see more of that power in action.

In addition, Gen Z's consumer behavior will not be limited to the generation itself. As they adopt new tools and display new behaviors, we will see those spreading to older generations. Youth culture in some ways is going mainstream. Just look at the history of social media. Facebook, which started as a platform of sharing between college students, spread over time to older generations—a maturation process that repeated itself with other networks. As Boomers and Gen Xers increasingly subscribe to the idea that "70 is the new 50" and are leading more youthful lifestyles, the Gen Z mindset is rippling upward.

This combination of *technology*, *values*, and *influence* will require brands, retailers, and other organizations seeking to engage the next generation, to develop a deep understanding of the interplay between these three elements and how they shape the ways Gen Z thinks and behaves.

My research identified four characteristics that form the foundation of who Gen Zers are as consumers. The four—seeking authenticity, celebrating individuality, consuming consciously, and navigating seamlessly between online and stores—stem directly from their values and the way they weave technology into their lives, and in turn, they are influencing new consumer trends or accelerating some we already familiar with (see Figure 9.1 and Table 9.1). Understanding these characteristics and their corresponding trends will be critical for brand and business leaders who want to effectively connect with the next generation.

Figure 9.1. Understanding the Gen Z Consumer: A Framework

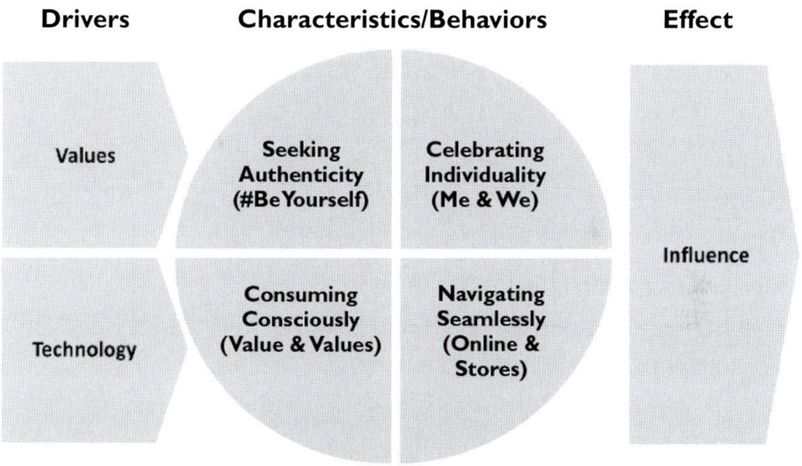

Drivers
Characteristics/Behaviors
Effect
Values
Seeking Authenticity (#BeYourself)
Celebrating Individuality (Me & We)
Influence
Technology
Consuming Consciously (Value & Values)
Navigating Seamlessly (Online & Stores)

Source: Gen Z Planet research

Table 9.1. Gen Z Consumers Characteristics and Related Trends

	Seeking authenticity	Celebrating individuality	Consuming consciously	Navigating seamlessly
What	Gen Z is preoccupied with being authentic and true to themselves. They expect brands to do the same. "Realness, honesty, and consistency" is what Gen Z wants brands to demonstrate.	Gen Z is all about standing out than fitting in to the point that they see themselves as brands. Yet that doesn't mean they disregard the collective, and they expect that brands will do the same.	Gen Z is financially conservative, prioritizing savings and remaining cautious with spending. But they will pay for and be loyal to brands that share their values and do good in the world.	Gen Zers don't make a distinction between physical stores and online stores. For them there is only *one retail* for which they have high expectations: constant stream of engaging content and unique experiences are just the start.
Why	Growing up in social media and celebrity culture, Gen Zers grew up to reject the overly polished and idealized images that pervade our society. Instead, they prefer to live by their mantra of #BeYourself. Lack of trust in traditional institutions and corporations have led Gen Zers to demand more authentic and truthful interactions with brands. Brand authenticity is the basis for Gen Z's trust.	Gen Z has a natural tendency to question norms and old societal constructs. They reject the idea that there is only one way of doing things or that there should be any "universal standards." They are creating their own. Since everyone is unique, everyone should be celebrated. The "we" for Gen Z is as important as the "me." Being the most diverse generation, inclusivity is one of their non-negotiables, and the need to belong to communities is strong.	Growing up during the 2008 recession and experiencing the economic effects of the COVID-19 pandemic, Gen Zers made financial security as one of their top priorities and a core value. Gen Zers grew up being exposed and highly tuned into social, racial, and environmental issues which shaped their core beliefs and values, affected their consumption behaviors, and defined their relationships with brands.	Growing up in a digital world, Gen Zers are accustomed to maneuver between touchpoints in a seamless way. Being spoiled for choice and having unlimited access to information and products, Gen Zers are looking for unique content and experiences that address their need for discovery and exploration.
Related trends	•Influencer marketing •The rise of "Z brands"	•Personalization •Inclusivity •Communities	•Re-commerce •Values-driven consumption	•Content is king •Experience is everything

Seeking Authenticity: #BeYourself

The word *authenticity* has been associated with Gen Z for quite some time and for a good reason—it is one of the most important characteristics of this generation. Therefore, to understand the Gen Z consumer, we must understand what authenticity means to them, why it became so important, and how it shapes their behaviors as consumers and their expectations from brands.

According to Dr. Michael Minervini, a New York–based psychologist, "Being true to one's own character is the essence of authenticity. It suggests an alignment between core beliefs and actual behavior—an alignment that is vital to our psychological well-being as humans." But internal alignment is just one part of the picture. We also seek to find alignment in the external world, which we achieve by constantly scanning those around us for what they say and do in order to determine whether we can trust them.

Authenticity fosters trust. When people behave authentically, others trust them. This is true for all types of relationships, including the ones we have with brands.

Gen Z grew up in a social media and celebrity culture, they saw their predecessors, the Millennials, turn to social media to create perfectly curated lives and have witnessed the ongoing debates on issues of identity and political correctness. As a result, Gen Z's quest for authenticity seems to be a natural reaction to what they view as a discrepancy between beliefs, talk, and actions. Amy, the 18-year-old from Pennsylvania, told me that she has gradually lost trust in what people post on social media because in her view: "People work too hard to show the more glamorous and appealing side of their lives or the cool things that they do . . . and it very quickly became unreal."

Indeed, "real" is what Gen Z wants. For them being authentic means having the courage to be themselves, as imperfect as they might be. Alexandra, also from Pennsylvania, told me that authenticity is one thing she looks for before following celebrities or other famous people: "I follow Cardi B on social media because I like her music, and I follow

B. Simone because she is funny, but the main thing I like about them is that the two of them don't hide their personalities. They are totally real."

Gen Z's appreciation of authenticity may explain the rise of platforms like TikTok, where users can just be themselves, forming an antithesis to the perfectly styled images that are being shared on other platforms. In fact, TikTok videos with the hashtag #BeYourself had over 1.1 billion views in mid-September 2020 (double of what it was six months earlier).

But Gen Z's quest for authenticity goes beyond their immediate circles as they seek to find an alignment between words and actions in the world around them, including in brands. When asked to evaluate different brand attributes, 67 percent of my research participants said authenticity is "important" or ""very important" when considering a brand. No other attribute was rated higher than that.

For a brand to be considered authentic, they feel it needs to be viewed as real, reliable, and transparent. They want brands to "be themselves," and they are constantly looking for that alignment between what a brand claims to be and what it actually does. The words *real, consistent*, and *honest* were the most recurring words Gen Zers used in interviews to describe brand authenticity. It is seen as a key attribute that eventually defines a brand's success. As one of my research participants put it: "a brand trying to be something they're not will ultimately fail." Being an authentic brand is about being true to who you are.

An example of such a brand is Aerie, the underwear lifestyle sub-brand under the umbrella of teen clothing retailer American Eagle Outfitters. In early 2014, understanding the immense pressure that young women have regarding how they look and how they feel about themselves, the brand launched its "aerie Real" campaign featuring models of all sizes in unretouched photos. In a statement that accompanied the launch, the company said, "The purpose of 'aerie Real' is to communicate there is no need to retouch beauty, and to give young women of all shapes and sizes the chance to discover amazing styles that work best for them. . . . We want to help empower young women to be confident in themselves and their bodies."[128] The message of empowerment, body positivity, and authenticity resonated not only because it has its own appeal but also because it was *consistent* with what the brand has always said about itself. The aerie Real campaign was just another demonstration of the overall brand message of inclusivity, optimism, and empowerment. Today, the brand's #AerieREAL Life website offers content on topics such as relationships, self-love, health and wellness, and discusses real-life issues, struggles, and happy moments that matter to the target audience. Oh and by the way, you can also click the "shop aerie" button and buy some clothes.

Authenticity pays off. Aerie has become one of the fastest-growing brands at a time when the apparel industry has been struggling. In the third quarter of 2019, the company reported that Aerie's comparable sales increased 20 percent, marking the twentieth consecutive quarter of double-digit sales growth.[129]

On the other hand, when an action doesn't align with a brand's stated values, it can backfire. Hallmark, for example, which has long been associated with family friendliness and celebration of life's milestones, states on its website: "Embracing diversity and inclusion is the best way to understand and serve our employees and consumers."[130] In 2008, the company was ahead of the game when they introduced same-sex wedding greeting cards at a time when most states did not recognize gay marriages. But just over a decade later, in response to pressure from a conservative group, Hallmark's TV channel pulled an ad by wedding planning company Zola that featured a same-sex couple kissing at their wedding. The ensuing backlash on social media forced the management to reverse its decision and find ways to rebuild trust with its consumers.

Trust has always been a precious commodity in the world of sales and marketing, and that's all the more true with Gen Z. As we saw earlier, 55 percent of Gen Z said they had little or no trust in corporations—a very high percentage for young individuals who just started their lives as independent consumers. Being distrustful is an integral part of who they are—perhaps because of their high degree of exposure to information and their ability to connect the dots and detect misalignments, hidden agendas, and self-serving statements.

However, as I have written a few years ago while at management consulting firm Kearney, just because consumers are low on trust doesn't mean that they entirely give up the need for a trusted authority. It just means that they have to look for information and guidance in different venues, which may help explain the rise of "influencers" as key agents in consumer's lives.[131]

When asked who influences their shopping decisions, 66 percent of Gen Zers cited their friends followed by family members, customer reviews, and social media influencers (see Figure 9.2). These four types of influences are viewed by Gen Zers as sources who have no agenda beyond sharing their views on a product or a service. More important, they are regarded as authentic and therefore trustworthy.

Figure 9.2. Purchasing Decision Influences

Q: Who influences your purchasing decisions?

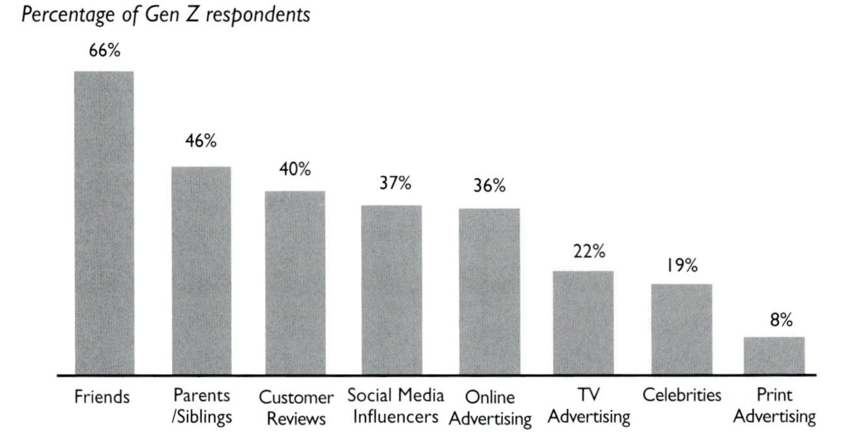

Source: Gen Z Planet research; N=1000

Until recently Gen Zers followed Millennial influencers, but in the past couple of years they have produced influencers of their own. For example, Emma Chamberlain, the YouTube star with over nine million followers, became known for her funny and authentic vlogs as well as for her unique editing style, which made her a celebrity among her teen fans. There is also Haley Pham, who shares her beauty transformations and dance videos with her two million followers, and TikTok stars like Charli D'Amelio (100 million followers and counting) and Jacob Sartorius (23 million followers).

Gen Zers like to follow influencers of their age because they can relate to them. They feel that these influencers share the same values and face similar challenges: juggling school and social life, experiencing first love, finding a summer job, or considering a student loan. It all goes back to one notion—authenticity.

Gen Z influencers can be an important marketing tool to win over the next generation, but brands must tread carefully. In the past few years, with the exponential growth in influencer marketing, some influencers became brands in their own right, charging huge sums for campaigns and social media endorsements, which resulted in consumer skepticism about their authenticity. A recent report by Takumi, the influencers marketing agency, found that 72 percent of consumers will unfollow an influencer for disingenuous endorsements.[132] Going forward, brands will have to be extremely selective in their influencer marketing approach and possibly rely more on "nano influencers"—those with a smaller number of followers who are still perceived by Gen Zers to be authentic and therefore trusted. In an interview, Annie Fong, Takumi's head of marketing, agreed:

> At Takumi, we've seen how nano- and micro-influencer marketing is one of the few ways brands can achieve sustainable growth in the new world of marketing. Whilst a macro-influencer is great for visibility and awareness, micro-

> influencers [are] truly able to push brand awareness out to their followers and deliver on the promise of connection by telling a story and engaging with their audience. With brands looking to work on building consumer loyalty, we are likely to see the demand for nano- and micro-influencers continue to grow. This is particularity true with Gen Z. The next generation of consumers want to see real people, saying it how it is and taking a much rawer approach that is closer to real life.

And if you needed any more evidence of Gen Z's demand for authenticity, look no further than a host of brands that are becoming popular with this generation. I call them "Z brands" because they were created with the next generation in mind. Similar to the influencer phenomenon, the rise of niche brands in the past decade was grounded in the declining level of trust in large corporations and brands and the increasing trust in small businesses. In my research, 85 percent of Gen Zers (and similar percentages of other generations) said they have a high level of trust in small businesses—a sentiment that made it possible for smaller brands to thrive.

But "Z brands" represent much more than just another niche or indie sector because they were created to address the specific needs of Gen Z: affordable prices and excellent value for money, standing up for causes that Gen Zers care about, and marketing that uses authentic communication and imagery that reflect Gen Z's lifestyle and culture.

One example is Billie, the direct-to-consumer razor brand that delivers shaving supplies and body care products designed for women. The brand offers quality razors in an array of colors and ergonomic designs at affordable prices. But its success has resulted not from the product alone. Billie is a brand with a message. Being vocal about the Pink Tax that is applied to feminine care products and about an industry in which women were an afterthought, the brand established itself quickly as a Gen Z favorite for both its authenticity and its mission. Their open conversation about body hair, the use of realistic imagery of models of all colors, and their commitment to donate one percent of their sales to women-related causes were all part of the appeal.[133] When Procter & Gamble attempted to acquire Billie in 2020 (a move that was blocked by the Federal Trade Commission), the company announcement indicated that access to Gen Z was one of the acquisition's goals.[134]

"Z brands" are not only popping up in the personal care spaces. They can be found in a variety of consumption categories, from fashion and beauty to food. Parade Underwear, Kinship skin care, and Impact Snacks are just a few examples. These, and other Z brands, present real challenges for established brands, who are faced with the strategic dilemma of whether to monitor these brands and eventually acquire them or create their own version of a "Z brand" to cater to this generation. One thing is certain: generic value propositions that are not tailored to Gen Z simply won't cut it with these demanding consumers.

Celebrating Individuality: Me *and* We

For most members of previous generations, their teenage years will be remembered, among other things, as a time when they wanted nothing more than to be like everyone else. They wanted to have the same fashionable shoes as their best friends and have the same toys that the kids next door played with. But starting with Millennials and now extending to Gen Z, that attitude seems to have changed.

Being different and unique is much more appealing to Gen Zers than fitting in. Over half (52 percent) of my research participants said they'd rather stand out than fit in, a figure that is slightly higher than Millennials (49 percent) but much higher than Gen X (36 percent).

My dream is to be an Instagram fashion influencer.

Dreamer: Olivia, 18, California

Artist: Betsy Huizi, 26, Xiamen, China

The need to stand out affects every aspect of their lives: the clothes they wear, the way they apply makeup, the hairstyles they choose, the way they show up on social media, the activities they participate in. It must be *different.* It must be *me.*

No single reason explains Gen Z's individualism. It is partially because of their upbringing in a culture that requires people from a young age to differentiate themselves in school or at work in order to get ahead. But it could also be because of the fact that compared to previous generations, Gen Zers have more tools, and they feel empowered, to do things in their own way.

Being unique, at its core, entails rejection of the idea that there is only one way of doing things or that everyone should follow the same standards. Of course, this is a challenging notion for global consumer brands that have spent decades and big dollars tirelessly spreading the idea of universal standards in beauty, fashion, tech, and other consumption categories to the point that it became hard to distinguish a consumer from Shanghai or Mumbai from their counterparts in New York or London. Consumer goods lost their local flavor as more consumers embraced the idea of global standards and more brands embraced the idea of scale.[135]

Gen Z, however, demands to be seen as unique and have their voices heard—and there was never a better time for that than now. Gen Zers are expressing their individuality by sharing their opinions, life stories, and preferences on social media. They are using the tools at their disposal to question norms and old social constructs and create their own, and they are forming a new age of creativity—an age where *everyone* is a designer, a photographer, or a curator. In fact, this is an age where everyone is a brand.

Having a personal brand is the ultimate form of individuality, and while the notion of a "digitally curated self" has existed for some time, gone are the days of the perfectly styled Instagram photos or Facebook feeds. Gen Zers, with their quest for authenticity and appreciation of individuality, allow the good and the bad, the ugly and the pretty, the lighthearted and the difficult moments to be shared in public in celebration of Me Inc. They spend hours painstakingly curating their presence on social media, ensuring they have the "right" persona on TikTok, LinkedIn, Snapchat, and other platforms. Lack of authenticity? Hardly! This is more of an act of savvy brand management, ensuring that they cater to different audiences with the right content.

If anyone has mastered personal branding, it would be Tiffany Zhong. At the age of 24, she is technically a Millennial, but she personally identifies more closely with Gen Z. She is the CEO of Zebra IQ, a company that helps brands better understand and connect with Gen Z. This role is a natural extension of her early career in Silicon Valley, where, straight out of high school, she became known as the youngest investor working for a venture capital firm. When we spoke, it was clear that for her, a personal brand is very real and very important: "It's all about conveying who you are—your expertise, your thought leadership, your insight, your reputation, and your network." Although she uses several platforms, Twitter is the place where she believes she can best connect with people who share similar interests, such as tech executives, investors, and founders. Therefore, she doubled down on her efforts to build her brand on that platform.

She is deliberate and thoughtful about what she shares online but also conscious that her followers expect her to always be authentic and on-brand. "I am very careful and conscious [of] how I come across. My personal brand right now is about Gen Z. I have experience helping investors and founders to understand youth culture, but if you asked me three years ago, the answer would have been different." According to Zhong, a personal brand is a dynamic concept that evolves over time, like any other brand.

She believes that Gen Zers today have no choice but to think about their personal brands. "Growing up with mobile phones and social media, Gen Zers understand from an early age the importance of how to present oneself." She particularly emphasizes the importance of reputation management. "Sometimes you can see influencers that get reprimanded because [of] things that they said years ago when they were kids. But the Internet doesn't care about that. If you made an inappropriate comment, it would come back to haunt you."

According to Zhong, "You can't just say everything that is on your mind." Having a personal brand comes with responsibility. For her, the best personal brands online are those who "simply focus on what they are passionate about, instead of crafting an unrealistic image." Having her own voice and sharing her passion for technology and innovation helped her build a growing community of 32,000 Twitter followers and counting.

By being their own brands, Gen Zers are creating a whole new dynamic in the relationships they have with consumer brands. Because they view customer relationships as a two-way street, Gen Zers want brands to have a conversation with them, not just talk at them. They want to be part of a brand—its product development process or its advertising campaign creation—and they want responses to their reviews and feedback. In addition, Gen Zers expect brands to give them the tools to evolve their personal brand and convey their uniqueness, a need that is driving an increased demand for personalization of both products and content. Personalization has become an important part of marketing in recent years, but it has not yet reached a level that satisfies the discerning Gen Z consumer. Sixty-nine percent of participants in a poll I conduced about personalization felt that the communications and interactions they have with brands are not as personalized as they would like, creating a big opportunity for brands.

Yet one should not conflate Gen Z's focus on individuality and uniqueness with a disregard for the collective. On the contrary; growing up as the most diverse generation and with the beliefs that everyone is unique and that everyone should be represented, they demand that brands be as inclusive and celebrate the "we." Whether it's brand advertising that reflects all gender expressions, races, body shapes and sizes, or products that reflect that diversity, Gen Z is spearheading the idea that acceptance of differences is the way to go.

In a poll gathering points of view on advertising, 78 percent of Gen Zers said they "agree" or "strongly agree" that brands have to be inclusive in their advertising and deliver their messages in a way that is authentic and respectful to the full gamut of their target consumers. The increased use of "real people" in advertising or the increased demand for gender-neutral products is partially a response to Gen Z's demand for more inclusivity.

Yet this is still an area where brands must make big improvements if they are to capture the potential of the Gen Z consumer. When asked how often they feel that they can "see themselves" in advertising or whether they can relate to the people depicted in the ads they see, 60 percent of the participants said they "never" or "rarely" feel this way—again, creating a major opportunity for brands.

Perhaps the most interesting aspect of the Gen Z consumer is where the "me" and the "we" intersect. The place where the need to express their unique voice is combined with their need to belong to something bigger than them—the community. According to the Pew Research Center, teens are very active members of online communities, participating in groups that center around hobbies, humor, pop culture, sports, fashion, politics, identity, and religion.[136] My own research shows that 39 percent of Gen Zers belong to brand communities. Their willingness and interest to take part in these communities offer brands a gold mine of opportunities to connect and build relationships with them.

Gen Zers love joining online and brand communities for a variety of reasons. Some are in it for the reward: "I am in a Starbucks group because I can rack up points and get rewards and free items." Others want to make a contribution to a brand they love: "I feel that my input helps brands become better." Some like having a sense of belonging: "It makes me feel like I am part of something." And some are in it for the learning: "It's a great way to learn new things. Listening to people who know a lot on a certain topic helps me think outside the box."

Brands can choose to collaborate with existing communities where Gen Zers congregate (think Twitch). That means having access to a highly defined audience and the ability to reach them with a more precise message. Alternatively, brands can create their own community by inviting Gen Z consumers who have passion for the brand to join in.

Consuming Consciously: Value *and* Values

Consider this statement from Jacob: "I always search for the best price I can get, but personally I do see sometimes the value in buying products that are a little bit more expensive that are going to last a little bit longer so I can give them to my brother or re-sell them online." Or, take Amy: "When I shop for clothing, I look for quality that I can wear for a long time. That's beneficial for the environment. I try to find good brands, reasonable price, fashionability, and quality."

Jacob and Amy sum up the essence of how Gen Z is evolving the notion of consumption, what they are looking for when they shop, and what they expect from brands.

As outlined in the previous chapter, Gen Z is financially conservative. Because they value financial security and prioritize savings, they are extremely cost-conscious, one could even say frugal. In my research, 80 percent of Gen Zers indicated that price is "important" or "very important" when making a purchase (see Figure 9.3), a figure that was slightly higher than Millennials and Gen Xers. To be clear, Gen Zers are not after the lowest price: they want the best value they can get for their money. To that end, they relentlessly conduct product searches before making a purchase and read customer reviews to ascertain other product attributes aside from price. A commanding 84 percent of the participants indicated that they search products online before making a purchase, and 80 percent indicated that they read customer reviews.

But value is only one part of the equation.

What really distinguishes Gen Z consumers from previous generations is their expectation that brands will reflect their beliefs and values and do something good in the world. Gen Zers want to align themselves with brands that have purpose, stand for something, and are willing to take a stance on issues that matter to them. And while standing up for something may mean different things to each consumer, Gen Zers seem to be united around environmental and social issues like equality and diversity.

Their price sensitivity combined with their environmental consciousness have already made a dent in the consumer world, as this combination is fundamentally redefining what ownership means. After watching the Millennials drive the "access over ownership" trend by renting clothes from Rent the Runway or furniture from LiveFeather, we now see Gen Zers take the definition of ownership to a whole new level, becoming a driving force behind the re-commerce trend, which in essence is "temporary ownership." For the pragmatic Gen Zers, buying, using, enjoying, and then reselling products makes perfect sense. By reselling an item, they can cover part of the purchase cost, or in the case of luxury goods, even make a profit sometimes. Equally important, they can make a positive impact on the environment.

No one understands this dynamic better than Depop, the re-commerce, peer-to-peer social shopping platform that has become extremely popular with Gen Zers in the United States and abroad. In my interview with Depop's CEO, Maria Raga, she attributed the company's success to the alignment between its core values—entrepreneurship, sustainability, and diversity—and the values that Gen Zers hold dear.

Depop users can buy old clothes from and sell them to other users and earn an income. Some do it as a side hustle and some are more deeply involved. "Entrepreneurship is about giving people an opportunity to be independent, which is the core value proposition of the platform," Raga said. "Gen Z is more entrepreneurial than previous generations.

They seize the opportunities afforded to them by technology and by social media, and as a result, they gain access to careers and financial opportunities that were harder to break into in the past."

The company's second value is sustainability. "By extending the life of the garment, every Depop user has an opportunity to make an impact, and the more we grow our business, the more impact we make," said Raga. Indeed, Gen Z is increasingly aware of the high environmental and social cost of consumption, especially of fashion products. It is hard for them to align with the long list of sins that are associated with the practices of the fashion industry, from failing to improve working conditions and wages in factories in poor countries to the environmental impact of dyeing, printing, manufacturing, and shipping garments all around the world only to end up with tons of clothes in landfills every year. Those costs make re-commerce an attractive option.

The company's third value is diversity, which according to Raga is all about "community, acceptance, and meritocracy"—three elements that foster trust and stronger emotional connection with the brand.

And while Raga recognizes that price consciousness is an important factor in Gen Z's purchasing decisions, she said that it's not only about price: "If it was about price alone, teens and young adults would have turned to deep discount stores to get the lowest possible price, but they don't. They want higher-quality items at affordable prices; they want the creative possibilities and self-expression that the platform offers, but as importantly they want to feel good about their consumption." The resale market is growing three times faster than overall retail.

My research identified similar themes. When asked what factors are important when making a purchase, quality topped the list. Higher-quality items can be used longer or resold (or both). In addition, consumers are increasingly paying attention to where and how products are made and what materials or ingredients are being used (see Figure 9.3). They look critically at brands that violate or fail to share their values, and they naturally gravitate toward and reward brands that have purpose and a mission that resonate with them.

Figure 9.3. Purchasing Decision Factors

Q: When making a purchase, how important are the following factors?

Percentage of Gen Z respondents who answered "important" or "very important"

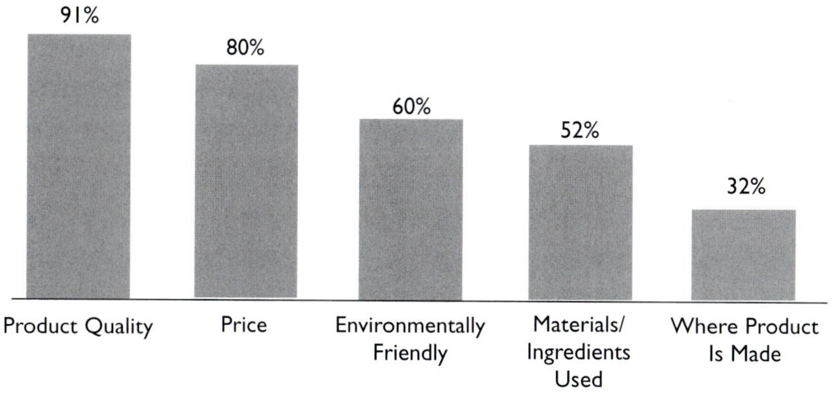

Source: Gen Z Planet research; N=1000

One such brand is Sand Cloud, an apparel and lifestyle company founded on the sunny beaches of San Diego with a mission to protect the oceans. The three founders, friends with a dream to reinvent the age-old beach towel, started the company in 2014. Committed to using sustainable materials and donating a portion of all sales to marine conservation charities, the three quickly discovered that their most engaged audiences were teens and young adults—Gen Zers.

"We realized that our brand and our mission resonated most with Gen Z. Partially because we launched on social media and that's where they are, but also because they do seek brands with a bigger purpose," said Brandon Leibel, co-founder of Sand Cloud. But purpose and words are not enough, as Gen Zers expect real action and on that front Sand Cloud has a lot to show. All of its products are sustainably made or serve as a way to live a sustainable life. Since producing that first beach towel, the brand has expanded into other eco-friendly accessories, like clothing made from yarn that is produced from recycled materials, reef-safe sunscreen, reusable glass water bottles, and reusable metal straws. All of the packaging is made from biodegradable poly matter.

Gen Zers, according to Leibel, "are very much 'on the ball' when it comes to assessing brands, advertising, and pricing. They understand when a brand is not transparent or is inauthentic. We try to be as transparent as possible about our products and the charities we support. For example, we let our nonprofit partners, post on our social media platforms and share their mission with our followers. We're living up to our word." Or, as their tagline says, #Savethefishes.

There is nothing that Gen Z likes more than brands that live up to their word, stand up for something, or make a positive impact on society. One case in point is Nike's decision to partner with Colin Kaepernick, the former NFL quarterback who kneeled during the national anthem to protest police brutality and racism toward Black Americans. The decision ignited both rage and support from consumers. Whether you liked it or hated it, you could not ignore it. Nike signaled clearly what they stand for, how they want to be seen, and which conversations they want to be part of. In my research, Nike tops the list of Gen Z's favorite brands.

According to a 2018 study by PR firm Edelman, nearly 60 percent of American consumers base their purchasing decisions on their political and social values, a remarkable increase of 13 points since 2017, and some of that increase can surely be attributed to Gen Z. The report concludes, "These 'Belief-Driven Buyers' will choose, switch, avoid or boycott a brand based on where it stands on the political or social issues they care about. Opting out of taking a stand is no longer an option for brands."[137]

Navigating Seamlessly: Online and In-Store

Much has been written over the past decade about the big changes that the retail industry is going through. The apocalyptic view pointed to slowing mall traffic, the rising number of store closures, and retailer bankruptcies. Headlines such as "the end of retail" and the "death of the store" became common and were further exacerbated by the effects of the COVID-19 global pandemic. The opposing view claimed that what we are experiencing is simply an evolution driven by consumers who seek a different type of shopping experiences and by technologies that enable retailers to deliver them.

The interesting thing is that both views are correct. "Dull retail" is pretty much dead and "experiential retail" is on the rise. So while the U.S. retail market is expected to see significant store closures in a post-pandemic world, the physical store will continue to live on, and Gen Z seems to hold the key to keeping it going for as long as it meets their expectations.

For a generation that is defined by technology, especially the smartphone, one would expect that Gen Zers would be e-commerce devotees. Yet they are showing a strong preference for shopping in physical stores, as these satisfy their need for community, experience, and direct interaction with brands. For Gen Z, shopping is a very social experience. Many of them go to stores with their friends or family members. "I am not crazy about online shopping," Marlene told me. "I like to go to stores. I prefer to see things in person and hang out with my friends." Indeed, 58 percent of my research participants said their favorite channel is stores, compared to 50 percent of Millennials who said the same. Even during the COVID-19 pandemic, 73 percent of those I polled said they are looking forward to go back to stores and expect to visit stores at the same frequency or even more often then they did before the pandemic. This does not mean that Gen

Zers don't shop online. They just turn to this channel for research and discovery purposes, and for convenience.

However, asking Gen Zers whether they like "stores" more than they like "online shopping" may not be a fair question. By asking them to choose a favorite, I was forcing on them my own point of view—one that separates physical stores from their virtual counterparts. Yet for Gen Z that kind of distinction does not exist. For them there is only one type of retail—the sum of all the touchpoints through which they interact with a brand or a retailer.

This notion of "one retail" has significant implications for retailers as it requires them to deliver products and services in a consistent manner across all their touchpoints. What's more, they have to do so in a way that attracts the attention of a generation known for its eight-second attention span.

To capture Gen Z's attention, it's important to understand where their shopping journey starts and where are they discovering new products and brands. The answer to these questions is overwhelmingly *online*. Ninety percent of my research participants said they discover new products and new brands on social media. By comparison, only 80 percent of Millennials and 54 percent of Gen X said the same. Only a small number of participants indicated print advertising as a source of product and brand discovery (see Figure 9.4).

Instagram scored the highest as a source of discovery, being favored by 84 percent of Gen Z. Yet there is no guarantee that it will remain this way. Gen Z attention is shifting constantly and quickly. In the past few years, they have adopted Snapchat and more recently taken to TikTok. Brands and retailers will have to be agile in understanding how Gen Z's attention shifts to ensure that they are advertising in the right place at the right time and that they are not missing important touchpoints. In the era of the Gen Z consumer, "follow the attention" is the new "follow the money."

Figure 9.4. Brand and Product Discovery

Q: Which of the following are your main sources for discovering new brands and products?

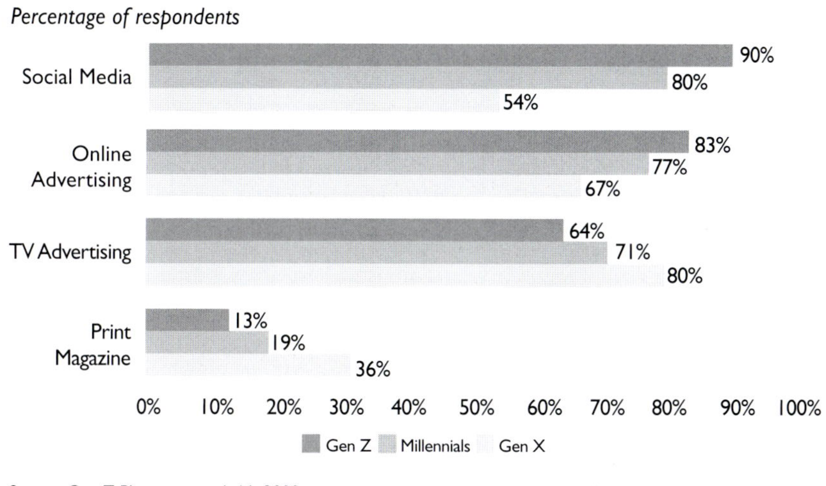

Source: Gen Z Planet research; N=3000

Still, in a highly competitive world that is flooded with brands, products, and information, following the attention may not be enough. My research shows that to resonate with the Gen Z consumer, brands and retailers will have to excel on two fronts: creating interesting *content* and producing engaging *experiences.*

When I asked what type of content they value most, participants commented: "I like content that comes from new musicians or artists . . . and original art or photography" or "I like stories of human kindness and inspiring quotes" and "stories about life transformation." Many mentioned specific topics of interest like body positivity, mental health, fitness, fashion, cars, and gaming. The pattern was clear: Gen Zers are interested in creative content, personal stories they can relate to and be inspired by, and content about issues that are top of mind to them.

Asked what would they do if a brand they follow on social media stopped sharing interesting content, some said they would "just scroll faster and ignore the content." Others, however, said they would take more drastic action: stop following the brand altogether and remove themselves from its mailing list. This is exactly the kind of the disruptive behavior that Gen Z is bringing to the table. They want to be constantly inspired and stimulated by brands; otherwise, they won't stick around. "Content is King" is no more a cliché, and it has huge implications for retailers and brands. It requires a finger on the pulse to first understand which content will resonate with Gen Z and then the capability to deliver content at scale in order to serve adequately every single touchpoint. Retailers and brands are in some ways becoming media companies. It is no longer just about "having the right product, at the right time, at the right place."

Beyond their unforgiving attitude toward content, Gen Z expectations continue to run high when they engage in retail transactions both online and in-store. When asked what is most important to them when shopping, price was the leading factors for both channels (see Figure 9.5). That is quite expected considering how cost-conscious they are. But following that, they stressed the importance of the experience. It is important to note that while the starting point for evaluating a store is price, when faced with a specific product selection, quality will trump price, as we saw in in the previous chapter.

For the in-store channel, unique merchandise was the second most important attribute, which is not a surprise considering Gen Z's preoccupation with individuality and uniqueness. It offers retailers an opportunity to cater to Gen Z by curating unique assortments in the form of limited editions, exclusive brands, or personalization options.

Customer service, overall atmosphere, and store design were the next most important attributes. These three features have evolved over the years to include technology, which is very appealing to a generation of digital natives. Gen Zers expect retailers to deliver services in a seamless and frictionless manner that truly enhances

Figure 9.5. Importance of Shopping Attributes by Channel

Q: What are the most important attributes when shopping?

Top five attributes selected by Gen Z (in order of importance)

In-Store	Online
Price	Price
Unique merchandise	Free shipping/returns
Customer service	Fast delivery
Overall atmosphere	Product availability
Store design	Site has customer reviews

Source: Gen Z Planet Research; N=1000

their shopping experience. In a poll inquiring about the desirability of various in-store retail technologies, self-checkout, free Wi-Fi and contactless payment topped the list, followed by interactive screens for product search and ordering and BOPIS (buy online, pickup in store). Surprisingly, "Instagrammable fixtures"—those designed specifically for photo taking and sharing—were the lowest on the list.

As for shopping online, Gen Z's expectations revolve around elements of cost and convenience such as free shipping and returns or speed of delivery. These were not much different from those of older generations.

Taylor, a 16-year-old from New York, was one of the few Gen Zers I met who has a preference for online shopping. Being a competitive rower, she is juggling her school commitments with training, which means that she has little time for or interest in going to stores. "I find going to stores to be very stressful and confusing," she said. "It is much easier to find things online." Lululemon and Amazon Fashion are Taylor's favorite online destinations, the first "for its quality and the consistency of the cut and fit" and the latter for "its selection, affordable prices, and speedy delivery."

Reacting to these expectations and behaviors, retailers in the past few years have invested heavily in store technologies, ramped up their online presence, increased investment in content marketing, and most importantly, started creating new retail concepts that are designed to appeal to a new generation of shoppers.

One example is Showfields, a New York City–based retail concept that is making waves in the industry. It is a store like no other. In fact, it's not really a store but a brand platform that was designed to take its customers on a journey of discovery. It all started when Showfields CEO and co-founder Tal Zvi Nathanel found that he enjoyed scrolling through Instagram posts more than strolling through retail stores. "Retail lost the 'discovery' element," he told me. "Yet there is so much to discover at a time when many digitally native brands are being launched and there are so many innovative and exciting products to be found."

Nathanel believes that "customers do not like to be sold to; they want to go through their own journey and move from being observers, to being participants and only then shoppers . . . consumers consciously or unconsciously, are driven by what they experience digitally every day: the personalization of Netflix or Spotify or the discovery on Instagram and they bring these expectations when they come to stores." This idea is at the center of the concept he created—a platform that combines carefully curated direct-to-consumer brands with art exhibitions, theatrical experiences, and community events that are created from the point of view of what customers want and allow them to explore and discover. The platform is both physical and digital, yet its founder doesn't make this kind of distinction: "When you start separating online and offline, you immediately lose relevance, because this kind of separation doesn't really exist. The only thing that matters is delivering the best experience in every customer touchpoint"—a perfect example of one retail.

As Showfields is reinventing the store experience, others are looking to do the same in the e-commerce space. Neha Singh, the CEO of

Obsess, is on a mission to reinvent the e-commerce interface through virtual stores and highly interactive virtual experiences. According to her, "The e-commerce interface that Amazon created twenty-five years ago to sell books is still dominating the online shopping experience, resulting in little differentiation for brands. As technology has evolved and Millennials and Gen Zers are seeking more experiential, fun shopping environments both online and in stores, there is an opportunity to rethink that interface." When we met, Singh had just launched her ShopObsess.co site, which contains virtual stores for the latest trends in fashion, beauty, and home. Each store sells brands and products that fit the values of the new generation of consumers: range of price points, sustainability, diversity, and inclusivity. Models of all sizes are shown together in every store, and there is no separate "plus size" section. The site covers everything that reflects the target consumer lifestyle, from athleisure and wellness to party supplies.

Similar to others in the industry, Singh doesn't see the physical store disappearing. Instead, she said, "Its format and purpose will change. Customer acquisition is cheaper in stores than online, especially in densely populated areas, and that will force retailers to reinvent the store. In parallel to that, with more advances in virtual reality technology and computer-generated imaging, online stores will become more real, more social, and more enjoyable."

So, when navigating seamlessly between various touchpoints, Gen Zers will navigate not only between experience and convenience but also between different experiences.

To sum up, the rise of the next generation will not mark the end of the retail store or a complete transition to online shopping. Instead they drive a shift toward a vision that makes no distinction between the two channels. How can a brand improve their marketing to capture the opportunities that this revolutionary generation brings? That is the challenge addressed in this book's final chapter.

Chapter 9: The 360 View

- Gen Z, with its distinct set of values, understanding of the power of technology, and ability to influence others, is set to accelerate the disruption already facing consumer brands and retailers.
- *Values* and *technology* are the main drivers behind four key consumer characteristics Gen Zers already display. These are: seeking authenticity, celebrating individuality, consuming consciously, and navigating seamlessly between online and physical stores. These four characteristics have already had a notable influence on the broader consumer market: creating new trends or accelerating ones we are familiar with.
- Authenticity is the cornerstone of building trust with a generation that constantly scrutinizes brands and holds them accountable for what they say versus what they do. Gen Zers are more likely to trust peers, influencers, and "people like them," forcing brands to create a more authentic representation of who they are and have a clear influencer marketing strategy.
- Gen Zers seek value *and* values. Affordable prices and good value for the money are keys to attracting these price-conscious consumers. But price alone is not enough. Gen Zers expect brands to stand for something that is bigger than their product, service, or profits and do something for the greater good.
- Individuality is core to who Gen Z is. They would rather stand out than fit in. As a result, Gen Zers expect brands to treat them as individuals requiring more personalized communication and products.
- As much as they care about the "me," Gen Z, the most diverse generation, cares also about inclusivity and celebration of the "we" and expect brands to do the same. Whether it's brand advertising that reflects all races, gender expressions, and body

shapes and sizes, Gen Z is spearheading the idea that acceptance of differences is the way to go.

- Perhaps the most important characteristics of the Gen Z consumer is where the "me" and the "we" intersect. The place where the need to express their unique voice is combined with their need to belong to something—the community. Communities are one of the best tools brands have to build followers and engage the next generation.
- Finally, is the way they shop. Gen Zers do not really distinguish between online and physical stores. For them there is only *one* type of retail—the sum of all the touchpoints through which they interact with a brand or a retailer.
- To serve the Gen Z consumer, retailers and brands will have to excel on two fronts: creating engaging content and experiences and delivering both in a consistent manner across all their touchpoints. Failing to do so will result in Gen Z taking its interest and dollars elsewhere.

My dream is to create a completely sustainable world to live in.

Dreamer: Grace, 19, Texas
Artist: Xuetong Wang, 24, New York, N.Y.

CHAPTER 10

Next-Generation Marketing

As the power of the Gen Z consumer continues to rise, and its ability to disrupt becomes more evident, brands will be required to deploy different marketing approaches to appeal to them. Next-generation consumers need next-generation marketing.

Based on the research presented in this book, I have identified six building blocks that form the foundation of next-generation marketing—a set of strategies and tactics that businesses should consider when they connect, engage, and build long-term relationships with Generation Z (see Figure 10.1).

The most important aspect of marketing to Gen Z is to maintain a human-centric approach in everything you do. "Think human" is the common thread across the six building blocks, as each one of them, regardless the tactics it deploys, caters to a core human need. Together they reflect Gen Z's desire for community and connection, self-expression, independent discovery, and higher purpose.

Figure 10.1. The Building Blocks of Next-Generation Marketing

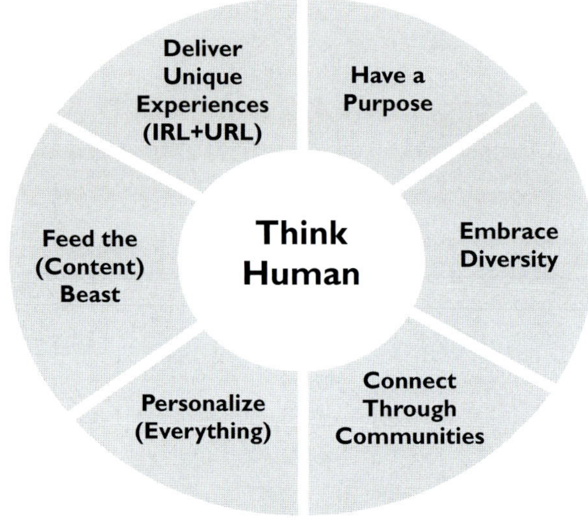

Source: Gen Z Planet research

This is not to say that older generations do not seek the same, but as we have seen throughout this book, Gen Z is much more vocal in demanding that brands address these needs.

This chapter outlines the six building blocks and provides some examples of how they are used by leading brands. It is intended to offer guidelines as opposed to providing a prescription. Each company will have to find the best way to use these building blocks, either individually or in combination with each other.

Building Block #1: Have a Purpose

Activism has become the hallmark of Gen Z. They tend to gravitate toward purpose-driven brands that reflect their values, and they expect brands to be committed to a cause. Moreover, they are willing and ready to exercise their purchasing power to support brands that are aligned with their values or boycott brands that don't. The values that are increasingly becoming purchasing decision criteria include environmental and social impact, health, wellness, and diversity. In recent years, these have translated into specific expectations from consumers in general, and Gen Z in particular, making "purpose" a business imperative.

In one of my polls of Gen Zers, 78 percent said it is important that brands have a purpose that goes beyond their sales and profits. "I generally feel better supporting brands that do something good in the world with the profit they make," wrote one participant. Another pointed to the fact that well-known brands have a platform and therefore "it should be their duty to raise awareness [to issues]" and provide support.

When defining their purpose, brands should consider first and foremost their ability to practice what they preach. To resonate with Gen Z, the choice of cause must be authentic and must be truly aligned with the overall nature of the brand and what it delivers to consumers. Think of Tesla and its mission to save the environment by increasing the use of electric cars, Dove's self-esteem and body confidence program that is directly linked to its body care products, and TOMS Shoes' donation of a pair of shoes to people in need every time they sell a pair.

By choosing and clearly communicating a cause, brands not only raise awareness of the issues they wish to support but also offer Gen Zers (and other consumers) a new form of social currency that comes from being associated with the brand.

However, whatever the cause is, brands must live up to the promise of their purpose. Paying lip service is not an option with Gen Zers. At a closed meeting with the press in June 2019, Alan Jope, then the newly appointed CEO of Unilever, cautioned:

> We're at a crossroads because there are too many examples of brands undermining purposeful marketing by launching campaigns that don't back up what the brand says with what the brand does. Green-washing, purpose-washing, cause-washing, woke-washing—call it what you will—it's bad for our industry. It is polluting purpose. We've all seen it and we know it when we

> see it. Fake purpose is dangerous. It threatens to further destroy trust in our industry when it is already in short supply.[138]

Gen Z loves brands that not only declare a purpose but are also willing to back it up with actions. Increasingly, they expect brands to take a stance on social and political issues, such as race or gun control. Fifty-eight percent of my poll's participants said it is important for a brand to take a stance on these or similar issues. Participants' comments included: "If big companies get behind actual problems in our society then that's when we'll be able to see an actual change that we need to see," "Tone-deaf companies don't survive," and "Popular brands should take a stance and help spread awareness about different topics that are serious and relevant to a large number of people." Of course, such views don't describe the entire generation. Forty-two percent of the participants objected to the idea mostly because they thought that taking a stance will alienate consumers who do not support the cause or that politics should not be mixed with business.

These expectations place brand marketers in uncharted territory. Traditionally, brands have avoided taking a stance on certain social or political issues in order to appeal to a broader audience. But as the discussions of these issues intensify, and as consumers, especially Gen Z, demand that brands show leadership, more brands are stepping into this territory, including big names like Walmart with its announcement to stop selling ammunition that can be used in military-style assault rifles, Nike with its ongoing support for racial injustice, and luxury brand Gucci, which brought its support for reproductive freedom to its runway show in 2019. In an interview with the *Washington Post* after announcing his company's support for fighting gun violence, Chip Bergh, CEO of Levi Strauss & Co., said, "It's inevitable that were going to alienate some consumers, but we can no longer sit on the sidelines and remain silent on the issue."[139]

Clearly, having a purpose and taking a stance are the new currencies of brand management, but not every brand is positioned to trade in them successfully. It takes clarity, courage, and ability to support a cause authentically.

Building Block #2: Embrace Diversity

Gen Zers reject any norm that limits how they define their identity or any view that disturbs their aspiration for social, racial, and gender equality. Being the most diverse generation, Gen Z wants to celebrate diversity in all its forms and feels that nothing stands in the way of their self-expression.

In this context, when you're marketing to Gen Z, diversity and inclusion are no longer "nice to have" but are "must have." Gen Zers want to see advertising that reflects the diversity they experience in their everyday lives, in their homes, schools, and communities. They want brands to be inclusive and deliver their messages in a way that takes into account the full gamut of their target consumers, be it race, gender, sexual orientation, dress size, or body shape. And while advertising that shows biracial families or gay couples is more common these days, Gen Zers are pushing toward even greater inclusivity and ask for it to be delivered in an authentic manner.

Using stock images of "perfectly styled" diverse models won't cut it with a generation that is savvy enough to see through it. In one of my polls, the overwhelming majority (82 percent) of Gen Z said they "agree" or "strongly agree" that it's important for a brand to use "real people" in advertising and to project a realistic image of both people and society.

In recent years, we have seen some brands making headway in this direction. Dove, Aerie, and Parade underwear all use real women in their ads. Beauty retailer Sephora even cast its own store employees in one of its holiday campaigns. Still, for the majority of brands and retailers, this is an area for improvement if they want to capture the potential of Gen Z consumers and stay relevant. Remember, 60 percent of Gen Z said they "rarely" or "never" are able to "see themselves" in advertising.

Another way to embrace diversity is to create products that truly appeal to the broadest audiences possible. One good example is Rihanna's Fenty Beauty launch of a foundation in 40 shades. It communicated a message of inclusivity by inviting customers with different skin tones to find a shade that perfectly matches their skin. The brand has become popular with Gen Zers not only because of the product itself but also because of its willingness to take a stance on the issue of inclusion.

One aspect of diversity that is more challenging for consumer goods and retail companies is gender neutrality. For years the industry designed, advertised, and sold products using gender-based segmentation as a key organizing principle. And while cultural perceptions of masculinity and femininity have been shifting for some time, the industry has still to catch up, and Gen Zers may be the driving force behind it. In one of my polls, 34 percent of Gen Zers said they prefer to buy gender-neutral products, reflecting their inclination toward fluid identity and their desire to not be defined by what they view as old societal constructs. Gender-neutral products, especially clothing, also present a "blank canvas" which individualistic Gen Zers can then mold to their own preferences.

Reacting to this demand, some companies have started to deliver products, packaging, and advertising that fit the bill. Examples include Chanel's Gabrielle unisex bag, H&M's first gender-neutral collection in 2019, and more recently Calvin Klein's launch of CK Everyone, a gender-free fragrance. Outside the fashion and beauty industries, Coca-Cola launched its "Dude or Diva" campaign, which encouraged teens to share on social media both the masculine and feminine sides of their personalities by picking specially designed cans,[140] and Mattel has come out with its first gender-neutral doll, which kids can dress in any way they choose.

While most consumer goods and retail companies have been slower to catch on, innovative concepts like The Phluid Project in New York City may be an example of what is possible. The Phluid Project, which started as a physical store before moving online, was the first gender-neutral store in the city. It was created by Rob Smith, a former retail executive who merged his passion for social justice, especially representation of LGBTQ+, with his profession as a fashion retailer. Smith told me that he wanted to create "a space, an experience, and a community that fully embraces and accepts his core LGBTQ+ customers for who they are—a place for folks of all gender identities and gender expressions." But even more important, Smith views The Phluid Project as a platform that "is committed to challenging boundaries with humanity and questioning old traditions that inhibit freedom and self-expression."

The concept has resonated well beyond its core audience with people who share similar values and with Gen Zers who according to Smith will accelerate the acceptance of concepts like The Phluid Project: "Generation Z is defined by social justice and authenticity. They reject gender binaries and refuse to be defined by others or be placed in a box. They desire places and experiences that allow them to be who they are, and it doesn't matter if it's gender, sexual orientation, race, or religion."

The industry's approach to fluidity and gender-neutral products is still evolving. Retailers and brands are aware of the demand for gender-neutral products, and while being somewhat hindered by operating models that are essentially gender-based, they can still participate in this space in a variety of ways. For example, by creating a stand-alone gender-neutral brand like Collusion, by British retailer ASOS, or The Ordinary, by beauty retailer Deciem. Other options are to launch capsule collections or limited-edition lines, as Equipment, the clothing brand, did in partnership with The Phluid Project, or carve out space in stores and online to give home to emerging gender-neutral products.

I wish that she loved me.

Dreamer: Amanda, 18, New Jersey

Artist: Giovani Ramos, 24, Sao-Paolo, Brazil

Building Block #3: Connect Through Communities

Despite their strong inclination toward all things digital, Gen Z craves human connection at work and at play. The next generation's need for belonging and their need for self-expression play important roles in their adoption of online communities and engagement with brands. Tapping into these needs, by building active and engaged communities, could provide major benefits for brands. As stated earlier, 39 percent of Gen Zers indicated that they belong to brand communities.

Brand communities are by no means a new concept; they have been around for years. Consider the cult followers of Apple in the early '90s, Harley-Davidson's die-hard community of riders, and of course, MINI car enthusiasts. But today the opportunities to create and benefit from brand-based communities are far greater, considering social media and other online tools that are available to brands that want to build loyalty, increase sales, and reduce service costs.

There are three important principles that make a brand or product-focused community a success, especially when it involves youth audiences.

First, remember that *the community should serve the consumer, not the other way around.* Communities bring together people who have shared interests who come to the community with the expectation of benefiting from it. These benefits could be as simple as exchange of information or as profound as human connection. Therefore, having a clear idea about the value that you offer the community members is crucial. Sales growth and cost reduction are the positive side effects of that value. The power of a community is perhaps most exemplified by brands like Glossier and Food52. Both brands originated from blogs with highly engaged communities of like-minded people interested in content about beauty and cooking, respectively. As these communities grew, it made sense to their founders to provide more solutions to their members by offering them products that met their needs. Both brands became immensely popular and successful. Glossier's valuation exceeded $1 billion in 2019,[141] and Food52 sold a majority stake in the company in a deal that valued it at more than $100 million.[142]

Second, *in a community, the members are in control of the conversation and the brand is listening.* Gen Zers join a community to be heard, so brands will have to embrace both the positive and the negative feedback that emerge from these conversations. In a world where everyone can share their views with millions of others, the idea of brand control is simply obsolete, while listening to feedback can open the door for product improvements, innovation, and true connection with consumers.

The idea of listening to consumers or incorporating their feedback into a campaign or a product development process is nothing new, but the speed at which consumer behaviors and preferences are changing increases the uncertainty that is associated with new concepts and products, making consumer feedback a necessity. Building an engaged Gen Z community to tap into can be a gold mine for brands seeking to gather input fast and reduce uncertainty. Just remember that when gathering feedback from your Gen Z community, you must get the experience right. They don't want to participate in traditional in-person focus groups or answer lengthy online surveys, but they would happily respond to gamified features that make feedback sharing and participation engaging and fun. Features that resemble the technologies that Gen Zers use in their everyday lives tend to resonate well with these tech-savvy consumers. Examples include: thumbs-up or thumbs-down icons, the use of chatbots instead of open-ended questions to create a feel of a real conversation, and questions that are phrased as a challenge like the one I used with my Book Panel: "Describe Gen Z in one word."

Finally, *active engagement is the foundation of brand advocacy.* Gen Zers join a brand community to feel that they belong to something and that they can influence the actions of the brand by offering feedback or by co-creating with the brand. A study by the IBM Institute of

Business Value and the National Retail Federation found that "a key element in attracting Gen Zers to a brand is understanding their desire to contribute to, be part of, and co-create with the brands they love. For example, 44 percent of Gen Z said that, if given the opportunity, they would like to submit ideas for product design or participate in a product review . . . and 36% would like to create digital content for a brand."[143] For a generation that has democratized creativity, their willingness to engage with brands in ways that show their creativity is one of the greatest opportunity brands have these days.

One brand that used consumer creativity to expand its highly engaged community online is watchmaker Daniel Wellington. One of the fastest-growing brands in its category, it grew from a company that started in 2011 with a modest investment of $15,000 to sales exceeding $200 million five years later.[144] The brand's success was built partly on its distinctive and simple design but also on a creative social media strategy. The brand encourages customers who own the minimalistically designed watches to take photographs of their watches in various locations, situations, or whatever their creative selves can come up with for the chance of being featured on their Instagram feed, tagged #DWPickoftheday. The brand has close to five million highly engaged Instagram followers and an impressive campus influencer program that further expands its Gen Z reach.

Building on creativity, brands can also invite Gen Z consumers to design products. Retailer Nasty Gal did that in collaboration with UNiDAYS, the discount app for students. Nasty Gal invited UNiDAYS users to take part in designing T-shirts for the brand, promising that the selected designs would be produced and sold carrying the name of their creators. "Fashion is a statement. Time to make yours," the invitation read. The competition sparked a wave of creativity with Gen Zers submitting original designs with the hope of becoming part of the brand's new collection. Laura Duff, the grand prize winner, commented on her experience: "This contest kickstarted me to design like crazy, expand my mind, and try new things; I am so thankful that UNiDAYS and Nasty Gal had this opportunity."[145]

Bringing Gen Z into your process, whether for a quick feedback on a concept or for a more elaborate product design effort, will increase your chances of success with this generation. Considering how empowered and independent Gen Zers are as consumers, co-creating with them at this early stage of their lives is an opportunity to form lasting relationships with them while having a positive impact on brand performance.

A study by the Product Development and Management Association (PDMA) pointed to the long history of unsuccessful product launches in the consumer goods industry, suggesting that 49 percent of consumer product launches fail.[146] So if co-creation helps move the needle on this metric even a little, why not give it a try?

Building Block #4: Personalize (Everything)

Catering to highly individualistic consumers means delivering personalized products, services, and communication. Having a personalized experience not only makes Gen Zers feel understood and valued by a brand, but it also supports their pursuit of individuality. Gen Zers are eager to put their mark on items they buy. It could be as simple as engraving their initials on a product or as complex as purchasing a completely customized item. Being occupied with building their own personal brands, Gen Zers are always on the lookout for new ideas and products that help them to express their individuality, and personalization is an important tool in building a loyal Gen Z customer base.

However, offering customized physical products poses a significant challenge for consumer brands and retailers who benefited for years from the economies of scale provided by mass production and mass distribution. Now, to accommodate mass personalization, companies must adjust their infrastructure by introducing greater flexibility across their supply chains—a task not for the faint-hearted. This challenge is exacerbated by competition from a growing number of new brands that build their businesses from scratch on the premise of personalization having the advantage of both low-cost infrastructures and agility. Curology is one example.

Founded by dermatologist Dr. David Lortscher, Curology is on a mission to make the most effective skin care accessible to everyone by offering private-clinic levels of care in an accessible format and at an affordable price. Their focus on acne solutions means that many of their customers are Gen Zers who are in their teens and young adulthood years. According to Fabian Seelbach, chief marketing officer of Curology, "Personalization is how Curology ensures product efficacy. By understanding each customer as an individual, diagnosing their specific skin challenges, we are able to pick the right ingredients at the right strengths to optimally treat each person and help them see the results over time." The service is delivered online by dermatologists and registered nurses, and the personalized product, which contains individualized ingredients, arrives in a customized bottle with the customer's name on it.

Curology's value proposition resonated well with Gen Zers —which Seelbach attributes to their digital lifestyle. "Gen Z is accustomed to customizing everything . . . the way they put together their travel itinerary, structure their free time, customize their social media feeds or create playlists. They have grown to understand the value of personalization and are willing to pay for it. Therefore, the way we deliver the service and the product is natural to them."

So, what makes personalization a success? Seelbach offers a few pointers. "First, you have to deliver true personalization." For Curology, the medical staff's expertise is the basis for the personalized product choices and prescriptions. Moreover, each person's ongoing care is handled by the same staff member, allowing personal relationships and trust to develop over time. "Second, never offer 'personalization for the sake of personalization.' It must be purposeful and must deliver real value, which for Curology, it is its products' efficacy. And third is the combination of business process and systems that allow you to deliver an innovative service at scale and at affordable prices." Indeed, without the right infrastructure, personalization makes little commercial sense.

In addition to their interest in personalized products, Gen Zers expect personalization to be an integral part of their interactions with the brands, whether these take place over e-mail, text, or website visits. In one of my polls, Gen Z participants revealed what's important to them. Personalized offers and discounts topped the list, followed by the expectations that brands will demonstrate an understanding of what content they are interested in. Next on the list was the expectation that brands use the knowledge they already have about the consumers such as past purchases to make relevant recommendations. Perhaps more interesting (and challenging) was the expectation to be recognized by a website once they log in and be served personalized product offers or content.

Understanding that personalization is a two-way street, 60 percent of Gen Zers said they would share more of their personal data in return for personalized communications and experiences. It is important to note that Gen Zers are not blind to data privacy issues. Yet they feel confident that their knowledge of technology and ability to modify and control which data they share gives them some protection.

In short, Gen Z is increasingly adopting an attitude of "show me that you know me," and raising the bar of what personalization means. And while many brands and retailers have upped their microtargeting game by using machine learning technologies and big data analytics, 70 percent of Gen Zers who participated in my poll felt that the communications and interactions they have with brands and retailers are not sufficiently personalized.

There is no doubt, personalization is a big opportunity and one that brands and retailers can benefit from. A McKinsey & Company study on personalization at scale suggests that "Personalization can deliver five to eight times ROI on marketing spend and can lift sales by 10% or more."[147]

My dream is to influence positively as many lives as possible.

Dreamer: Haley, 20, North Carolina

Artist: Selma Nached, 21, Damascus, Syria

Building Block #5: Feed the (Content) Beast

Curiosity is a key behavioral driver. Everyone likes to explore and discover, and Gen Z is no different. But for a generation that grew up with instant access to information, exploration is part of their everyday life and they expect brands to satisfy their need for discovery through relevant and inspiring content.

From showing how products are made to providing practical tips or sharing brand-relevant stories, companies have plenty of opportunities to engage with Gen Z. For example, Dior shared the behind-the-scenes process of making the wedding dress for mega-influencer Chiara Ferragni, offering a window into the artisanal process of making a beautiful custom-made dress by an iconic brand as well as providing inspiration to many young brides to be.

Educational content is another way of fostering exploration and engagement that Gen Z particularly loves. This can be as simple as the how-to videos that have become extremely popular with Gen Z, covering everything from makeup tutorials to photography tips. But it can also be more elaborate, such as Bank of America's efforts to improve financial literacy by delivering financial education content in an engaging and accessible way. Educational content can also come in the form of articles that offer help on specific topics and are in line with the brand's mission. For example, a beverage brand might offer tips for throwing a party, an outdoor equipment brand might provide "backpacking 101" advice for travelers, and a fast-food chain might offer nutrition guidance. Educational content pays off because of its potential to shorten the sale cycle and build trust. A study by Conductor, a technology platform that helps companies to optimize their content, found that consumers "are 131% more likely to buy from a brand immediately after they consume educational content at the early stage of their purchasing journey and that there was 8% increase in viewing the brand as trustworthy one week after reading this content."[148]

Yet, considering that every Gen Zer is active on at least five social platforms and that they expect fresh content on each one of them, all the time, brands are faced with the daunting task of constantly having to create new content. The sheer volume that is needed to satisfy the need for exploration can be overwhelming. And as more consumers adopt the Gen Z mindset, brands will have to gear up their content production capabilities to win in a world that requires rapid, high-volume content creation.

Constantly feeding the content beast on social media channels has its obvious advantage of massive reach, but it's not risk-free. One risk brands face with marketing to and interacting with Gen Z via social media and other online intermediaries is that the data on consumer attention (where consumers are spending their time) often no longer resides with or belongs to the brand.

Today, Google, Amazon, Facebook, Netflix, and other tech companies know more about consumer behaviors than any individual brand knows. In other words, these companies have the advantage of knowing not only what a given consumer is doing vis-à-vis a single brand, but also how they behave across brands—which these tech giants have turned into a competitive advantage. For example, by understanding the viewing habits and interests of its members, Netflix has successfully launched its own programming because they knew how people consumed movies and therefore could cater to these tastes. On the physical product side, Amazon has leveraged its data to identify specific consumer needs, using its insight to launch its own products, enter new categories, and disrupt industries.

Zach Schwitzky, co-founder of Limbik, a tech startup that is using video data to improve the effectiveness of the creative process, told me: "We are living in an age of attention inequality, and the data advantages that some companies have means that, for example, Facebook could use its data to inform a hotel brand that rivals the biggest and best in the world, but no hotel chain could replicate the scale and community required to compete with the data Facebook has."

The question is, then, what should brands do to ensure that their most valuable assets—consumer attention and hence data—remain at least partially with the brand? This question is particularly important because of the significant amount of time Gen Zers spend on various platforms. Schwitzky believes that a brand's strategy needs to be a combination of "following the attention" and "becoming a destination": "You have to follow the attention and be where the crowd is, but also start giving consumers reasons to come back to your site or to your store, so you own the data," he said. "Disney has taken their content off Netflix—a move not everyone can afford. On the flip side, what is the risk of not acting? Will your brand exist in 10 years if your consumer attention and data are owned entirely by someone else?"

To become a destination, brands can deploy various strategies. For example, they can provide unique experiences or exclusive offerings that are available only through the brand's website or stores, thereby encouraging consumers to return to them. Another strategy is to create "destination content"—an exclusive form of content that is designed to truly add value to consumers. One example that comes to mind is Yummly, a platform owned by appliance maker Whirlpool. Yummly's mission is "to be the smartest and most helpful food platform in existence . . . by improving life in the kitchen for millions of home cooks around the world."[149] The platform, which has 26 million users and a depository of over two million recipes, is a gold mine for understanding how people plan meals, how they cook, and therefore how you create products to help their everyday lives. Another example is L'Oréal's MakeUp.com, a site with over 1.2 million followers across various platforms. It offers everything beauty consumers could look for: looks, tips and tutorials, videos and tips from influencers, and articles about various beauty topics. It is an online magazine with an option to make a purchase—instead of an advertisement that is focused only on making a sale.

Becoming a destination requires content that commands attention. This is especially important with Gen Zers, who can be hard to please but according to Schwitzky it's an investment worth making: "The ROI of trackable attention is [that] your business will still exist in five years."

Building Block #6: Deliver Unique Experiences (URL+IRL)

Welcome to Jeju Island, a world natural heritage site, with its endless green tea fields that stretch to the horizon. Volcanoes, waterfalls, vibrant wildlife, and beautiful sunsets have made the island a favorite holiday and travel destination. But you do not really have to travel all the way to South Korea, where Jeju Island is, to enjoy the benefits of its beauty. Instead, just step into one of Innisfree's stores around the world. Innisfree is a Seoul-based global beauty brand and maker of a wide range of skin care and makeup products. Using natural ingredients that are responsibly sourced from Jeju Island, the brand promotes green living in a creative and engaging way.

Upon entering an Innisfree store, customers step into Jeju's atmosphere. They are welcomed by walls of green living plants, the music of birds chirping or waves crashing, and the brand's signature scent in the air. They walk on floors resembling the rocks on the island as they navigate through the various store displays and products. The stores were designed for what Julien Bouzitat, who oversees the Innisfree brand in the United States, calls "discovery and playfulness."

Supporting the discovery are stations where shoppers can test the products. For example, in the hair care section, at the back of the store, shoppers can pour a product, mix it with water, create foam, smell it, and wash their hands, "a private experience that almost resembles your home bath." Playfulness is conveyed through both store design and entertainment. "Makeup is like a candy land," Bouzitat told me, describing the section where shoppers can interact with the product and use digital tools to create their own foundation, or shop for sheet masks out of vending machines. One of the highlights, offered at this point only in its Asian stores, is its virtual reality experience. You can choose between a "flying bicycle" that takes you for a flight over Jeju Island or you can be reduced to the size of an ingredient and learn how it travels from the fields through the island until it becomes part of the final product. In some locations, the brand also offers coffee shops that serve healthy drinks made from local ingredients like those used in the products.

At the core of all these experiences is the brand's purpose. "Our inspiration comes from Jeju," Bouzitat told me, "and [so] our number one priority is to maintain the ecosystem of the island and preserve it. Innisfree's parent company, Amorepacific, has a comprehensive preservation program of replanting trees on the island, cleaning its beaches, maintaining the green tea farms, and supporting local farmers, mostly women, from whom they source the Camellia flower, a key ingredient in our products." In addition, the brand has a comprehensive recycling program. Customers are invited to return empty plastic bottles in return for loyalty points. The plastic bottles are then transformed into other materials used by the brand in store merchandising.

Innisfree is just one example of how brands are gearing up to serve the next generation of consumers, for whom the experience is often more important than the product itself as it acts as a source of learning and discovery, creation of memories, and social currency.

Davide Bolis, CEO of 4EON, an experiential marketing agency, told me that Gen Z wants experiences that are authentic, cool, memorable, and shareable. "Gen Z likes to share what they do with their community," he said. "Social currency matters and participating in a 'cool' experience is as valuable as having the latest gadget, sometimes even more."

For a generation that can access utility and convenience anytime anywhere, brands have to create something unique and offer something extra both in real life (IRL) and online (URL). No matter what approach a brand chooses, the kinds of experiences that resonate with Gen Z are increasingly immersive.

Immersive experiences have become hot topics for brands in recent years and for good reason. In a world where people, especially the highly connected Gen Zers, are constantly exposed to marketing messages that can be easily filtered out, immersive experiences, especially those using technologies like augmented reality (AR) and virtual reality (VR), offer a whole new way for the consumer to feel in control, to explore at their own pace, and to take center stage in the story or the brand adventure. As Bolis said, "Gen Zers want to be the protagonist."

Saying that, you dont really need the latest and greatest technology to make your customers feel that they are the protagonists. Creativity and resourcefulness can go long way with Gen Z. Several examples which illustrate that point come to mind.

The first is JetBlue that in 2016 launched its first direct flight from New York to Palm Springs. To promote the new destination to New Yorkers in the middle of the winter, they placed prizes inside a giant block of ice in Madison Square Park and told passersby that if they could break through the ice, they could win the prize. Passersby enthusiastically used whatever they had to chip the ice and claimed everything from beach clothing and golf clubs to free tickets to Palm Springs. A social media campaign that ran in parallel helped magnify the effect for the airline.[150]

Another example is European beer brand Desperados and their "Epic Parties Imagined by You" campaign in which the brand "looked to consumers to ignite their party spirit by collecting their ideas and bringing the most epic ones to life."[151] One of these events, themed "unplugging," had partygoers swap their phones for a beer as they entered the party. The phones then linked together to create a video light show synchronized with the music. "Stop scrolling, start dancing" was the natural tagline as the brand allowed its consumers to disconnect from their phones, take part in a creative adventure, and enjoy the party.

The core idea behind offering unique experiences is placing the customer at the center. Great experiences are designed from the point of view of the consumer and allow them to move from a position of passive observers to active participants. Active participation—being a protagonist in a virtual reality experience, solving a challenge, or creating a piece of art—is the basis for engagement, stronger emotional connection with the brand, positive memorable impression, and amplification. Customers who go through a great experience are more likely to talk about it, share it with their social media followers, and become brand advocates.

So there you have it! The six building blocks of the next-generation marketing are all about giving Gen Zers the opportunity to be part of the brand conversation and contribute to the brand process while recognizing their needs for human connection, discovery, and higher purpose.

Chapter 10: The 360-View

There are six building blocks that form the foundation of marketing to Gen Z and they have one thing in common—a human-centric approach as they reflect Gen Z's desire for higher purpose, community and connection, self-expression, and independent discovery. The six building blocks are:

- **Have a purpose**: Gen Z gravitates toward purpose-driven brands that reflect their values, and they expect brands to be committed to a cause. Clarifying your brand purpose and delivering it in authentic manner is the starting point in winning the hearts and minds of Gen Z.

- **Embrace diversity**: Being the most diverse generation, Gen Z wants to celebrate diversity in all its forms. When marketing to Gen Z, diversity and inclusion are no longer "nice to have" but are "must have." Gen Zers want to see advertising that reflects the diversity they experience in their everyday lives and products that cater to the broad gamut of who they are.

- **Connect through communities**: Despite their strong inclination toward all things digital, Gen Z craves human connection at work and at play. Their need for belonging and their need for self-expression play important roles in their adoption of online communities and in their willingness to engage with brands. Forming a Gen Z community to either garner feedback or co-create with Gen Zers is one of the most powerful tools available to brands who want to win the next generation of consumers.
- **Personalize (everything)**: Catering to highly individualistic consumers means delivering personalized products, services, and communication. Having a personalized experience not only makes Gen Zers feel understood and valued by a brand, but it also supports their pursuit of individuality.
- **Feed the (content) beast**: Gen Z grew up with instant access to information. Exploration is part of their everyday life and they expect brands to satisfy their curiosity and need for discovery through relevant and inspiring content. From brand stories to educational and destination-content there are plenty of ways to cater to this need.
- **Deliver unique experiences**: Gen Z wants experiences that are authentic, cool, memorable, and shareable. The core idea behind offering unique experiences is placing Gen Zers at the center and enabling them to move from a position of passive observers to active participants. Active participation is the basis for a stronger emotional connection with the brand, positive impression, and amplification.

These six building blocks are intended to offer guidelines as opposed to provide a prescription. Each company or brand will have to find the best way to use these building blocks either individually or in combination with one another.

Conclusion

IN THE FEW years that have passed since I embarked on this journey of better understanding the next generation, Gen Z has risen to show its effect on multiple fronts. Their activism has become more visible. Their position as culture creators has grown stronger, and their potential to influence both work and commerce has become clearer.

They have marched for climate change, won Grammy Awards, monopolized TikTok with their lighthearted, humorous videos, and rallied their peers and adults around issues ranging from social justice to gender equality. They have also sparked moments of tension such as when the "OK Boomer" video went viral, indicating that as much as we like to talk about a "post-generational" world, there is still a need to build bridges. And there are internal tensions too, like the one we saw when conflicting views on how to handle speech on campuses burst into riots at UC Berkeley, highlighting one of the challenges this generation is grappling with—reconciling their values of radical inclusivity with protection of free speech.

Other moments have provoked mixed emotions, as when we virtually cheered the class of 2020 whose members graduated in the middle of a global pandemic, encouraged by their achievements but concerned about their uncertain future and career prospects.

Watching them rise, one thing became clear. Gen Z is here, and it cannot be ignored. As they gain cultural, economic, and political power, their voices will become louder, and *we* must listen.

This book in many ways has been an exercise in listening to what this generation has to say. In the process I learned that they are different and that they are going to be more demanding employees and consumers than we have ever seen before. Yet they come with a promise of questioning the world around them and by doing so potentially driving fundamental changes to it. In some ways, they have to.

Every generation has dealt with its own challenges—wars and famines, pandemics, economic booms and busts—but Gen Z is facing challenges that are global in nature: climate change, global health, wealth inequality, and significant levels of global debt. Meeting these challenges requires collaboration among nations and among people, and Gen Zers, who made community and connectivity their hallmarks, are willing to tackle these challenges, as is evident by their level of engagement and by some of the actions they have already taken. Even in the midst of the pandemic, 69 percent of Gen Zers said they are optimistic about the future despite the immense toll the pandemic has taken on their education, finances, and social lives. Yes, their ability to adapt and forge new paths is remarkable.

The question now is: are you and your organization ready to adapt to them?

If you are an employer, Gen Zers are your future talent and future leaders. Their values, their life experiences, the way they communicate, live, and work will make a mark on the workplace. Whether it will be a stormy ride or a smooth sail will depend on your willingness to prepare and adapt. Here are some questions to think about:

- Are you ready to offer Gen Zers the opportunities and the working conditions they are looking for?
- Are you willing to redesign your entry-level roles to benefit from their eagerness to learn and their willingness to share their digital chops with older generations?
- Are you open to having difficult discussions about generational tension?
- Are you willing to engage in a conversation with a generation that asks, "Why we do things this way" without the answer being "Because that's how we did it for fifty years"?
- Are you willing, and do you have what it takes, to attract, train, and develop a new generation of employees and equip them with the work and leadership skills that are needed for a 21st-century workplace?

If you are a marketer, you already know that Gen Z purchasing power presents an immense opportunity, but you also know that their purchasing behaviors might be a threat to your brand no matter which product or service you are selling. As we saw in this book, Gen Z is already changing the landscape of the consumer market. Gaining their trust and loyalty, as elusive as they might be, will depend on your willingness to adapt. Here are some questions to think about:

- Does your brand stand for something and do you have the receipts to show for it?
- Are you communicating with authenticity? Can you pass Gen Z's "B.S. test"?
- Do you have the capabilities that are required to follow their attention and ensure that you are at the right place at the right time with the right message?

- Do you have a "well-oiled content machine" that is capable of producing content that meets the expectations of this generation and does it at the speed they consume it?
- Do you understand the "formula" behind Z brands—those emerging brands that were created for Gen Z and are likely to take small (or big) bites in the market from established brands like yours?
- Do you have a Gen Z co-creation community?
- Are you top of mind? Are you a "Z destination"?

Being able to answer yes to all these questions is possibly unrealistic at this point. It is still early days. But using these questions to guide your preparedness is a good starting point. Being prepared for Gen Z and the way it is going to change our culture, work, and commerce increases the chances of winning their hearts and minds and of winning in general. Those who are not prepared will struggle to succeed in this fast-changing world. In a way, keeping up with Gen Z is keeping up with the world.

I hope this book gave you a better understanding of this fascinating generation that in a very short time has become an important voice of hope for our future and that you will use this insight to better relate to them in everything you do.

My Biggest Dream. . .

That one day people wake up and realize that we ourselves are the only ones to save this world (by our actions).

Maria, 18, Texas

Help humanity advance.

Jonathan, 17, New Hampshire

To live a fulfilling life so I can say I had little to no regrets.

Anthony, 18, Arizona

To write the next great American novel.

Jack, 17, Minnesota

To influence everyone I meet to be the best that they can be.

Samuel, 17, Kansas

I wish that after this global pandemic the world will realize what is important so we can all move forward toward greater progress!

Dreamer: Madison, 18, Florida

Artist: Alex Krugli, 33, Novi-Sad, Serbia

BOOKS

Notes

Introduction

1. Greta Thunberg, "Our House Is on Fire!" special address at the annual meeting of the World Economic Forum, January 25, 2019, YouTube, https://www.youtube.com/watch?v=M7dVF9xylaw.

2. "The Fourth Industrial Revolution, World Economic Forum, Davos 2019," YouTube, https://www.salesforce.com/au/video/4697312/.

3. Elizabeth Entenman, "Here's the Full Transcript of Emma Gonzalez's Passionate Anti-Gun Speech," Yahoo.com, February 17, 2018, https://www.yahoo.com/lifestyle/apos-full-transcript-emma-gonzalez-020405208.html.

4. March for Our Lives, Wikipedia, https://en.wikipedia.org/wiki/March_for_Our_Lives.

5. "Our Story," SafeWander website, https://www.safewander.com/about.

6. Rakhi Chakraborty, "Shubham Banerjee, the World's Youngest Entrepreneur to Receive VC Funding, on His Life Changing Invention," YourStory, November 14, 2014, https://yourstory.com/2014/11/shubham-banerjee-vc-funding/.

7. Development Dimensions International, The Conference Board and Ernest & Young, "Global Leadership Forecast 2018," https://www.ddiworld.com/research/global-leadership-forecast-2018.

8. Isha Thorpe, "15 Times Beyonce Broke Records and Made History," iHeart Radio, May 29, 2020, https://www.iheart.com/content/2018-02-12-15-times-beyonce-has-broken-records-and-made-history/.

9. Christopher Kurz, Geng Li, and Daniel J. Vine, "Are Millennials Different?" Finance and Economics Discussion Series 2018-080, Board of Governors of the Federal Reserve System, Washington, D.C., November 2018, https://doi.org/10.17016/FEDS.2018.080.

Chapter 1: Who Is Gen Z?

10. Pew Research Center, "The Whys and Hows of Generations Research," September 3, 2015, https://www.pewresearch.org/politics/2015/09/03/the-whys-and-hows-of-generations-research/.

11. William Strauss and Neil Howe, *Generations: The History of America's Future* (New York: William Morrow, 1991).

12. Pew Research Center, "Whys and Hows of Generations Research."

13. Pew Research Center, "Whys and Hows of Generations Research."

14. Adapted from various sources including The Pew Research Center, "Whys and Hows of Generations Research"; Neil Howe, "Meet Mr. and Mrs. Gen X: A New Parent Generation," American Association of School Administrators, https://www.aasa.org/SchoolAdministratorArticle.aspx?id=11122; Mark McCrindle, "*The ABC of XYZ: Understanding the Global Generations,*" McCrindle Research, Gen Z Planet Research.

15. U.S. Census Bureau, Population Division, "Projected Race and Hispanic Origin: Main Projections Series for the United States, 2017–2060," 2018. https://www.census.gov/data/tables/2017/demo/popproj/2017-summary-tables.html.

16. D'Vera Cohn, "It's Official: Minority Babies Are the Majority among the Nation's Infants, But Only Just," Pew Research, June 23, 2016, https://www.pewresearch.org/fact-tank/2016/06/23/its-official-minority-babies-are-the-majority-among-the-nations-infants-but-only-just/.

17. William H. Frey, *Diversity Explosion: How New Racial Demographics Are Remaking America* (Washington, D.C.: Brookings Institution Press, 2018), ch. 1.

18. Kim Parker and Ruth Igielnik, "On the Cusp of Adulthood and Facing an Uncertain Future: What We Know About Gen Z So Far," Pew Research Center, May 14,2020, https://www.pewresearch.org/social-trends/2020/05/14/on-the-cusp-of-adulthood-and-facing-an-uncertain-future-what-we-know-about-gen-z-so-far-2/.

19. Kim Parker, Nikki Graf, and Ruth Igielnik, "Generation Z Looks a Lot Like Millennials on Key Social and Political Issues," Pew Research Center, January 17, 2019, https://www.pewresearch.org/social-trends/2019/01/17/generation-z-looks-a-lot-like-millennials-on-key-social-and-political-issues/.

20. Integrated Postsecondary Education Data System, "Use the Data," National Center for Education Statistics, https://nces.ed.gov/ipeds/datacenter/Data.aspx, Gen Z Planet Analysis.

21. *Leave It to Beaver,* "Family Scrapbook," June 20, 1963, https://www.imdb.com/title/tt0827865.

22. U.S. Census Bureau, "Living Arrangements of Children Under 18 Years and Marital Status of Parents, by Age, Sex, Race, and Hispanic Origin and Selected Characteristics of the Child for All Children," Table C3. https://www2.census.gov/programs-surveys/demo/tables/families/2017/cps-2017/tabc3-all.xls.

23. Pew Research Center, "Parenting in America: Outlook, Worries, Aspirations Are Strongly Linked to Financial Situation," December 17, 2015, https://www.pewsocialtrends.org/wp-content/uploads/sites/3/2015/12/2015-12-17_parenting-in-america_FINAL.pdf.

24. U.S. Census Bureau, "Living Arrangements of Children Under 18 Years and Marital Status of Parents, by Age, Sex, Race, and Hispanic Origin and Selected Characteristics of the Child for All Children," Table C3.

25. U.S. Census Bureau, "Living Arrangements of Children Under 18 Years and Marital Status of Parents, by Age, Sex, Race, and Hispanic Origin and Selected Characteristics of the Child for All Children," Table C3.

26. N. V. Pilkauskas and C. Cross, "Beyond the Nuclear Family: Trends in Children Living in Shared Households," *Demography* 55, no. 6 (2018): 2283–2297, https://doi.org/10.1007/s13524-018-0719-y.

27. Pew Research Center, "Parenting in America: Outlook, Worries, Aspirations Are Strongly Linked to Financial Situation," December 17, 2015.

28. U.S. Census Bureau, "U.S. Census Bureau Releases CPS Estimates of Same-Sex Households," November 19, 2019, https://www.census.gov/newsroom/press-releases/2019/same-sex-households.html.

29. Shoshana K. Goldberg and Kerith J. Conron, "How Many Same-Sex Couples in the U.S. Are Raising Children," Williams Institute, UCLA School of Law, July 2018.

30. Neil Howe, "Meet Mr. and Mrs. Gen X: A New Parent Generation," American Association of School Administrators, https://www.aasa.org/SchoolAdministratorArticle.aspx?id=11122.

31. Matthias Doepke and Fabrizio Zilibotti, *Love, Money, and Parenting: How Economics Explains the Way We Raise Our Kids* (Princeton, N.J.: Princeton University Press, 2019). A permission to reprint was conveyed through Copyright Clearance Center.

32. Elka Torpey, "Measuring the Value of Education," U.S. Bureau of Labor Statistics, April 2018, https://www.bls.gov/careeroutlook/2018/data-on-display/education-pays.htm.

33. Doepke and Zilibotti, *Love, Money, and Parenting.*

34. Russell Freedman, *Children of the Great Depression* (New York: Clarion Books, 2005).

35. G. Carlo, L. M. Padilla-Walker, and R. Day, "A Test of the Economic Strain Model on Adolescents' Prosocial Behaviors," *Journal of Research on Adolescence* 21, no. 4 (2011): 842–848.

36. Katherine Schaeffer, "6 Facts about Economic Inequality in the U.S.," Pew Research Center, February 7, 2020, https://www.pewresearch.org/fact-tank/2020/02/07/6-facts-about-economic-inequality-in-the-u-s/.

37. U.S. Census Bureau, "Selected Measures of Household Income Dispersion: 1967 to 2018," Table A-4. https://www.census.gov/data/tables/time-series/demo/income-poverty/historical-income-inequality.html.

38. American Psychological Association, "Stress in America™: Generation Z," October 2018, https://www.apa.org/news/press/releases/stress/2018/stress-gen-z.pdf.

39. Ryan M. Niemiec, "Gen Z: A Strong Generation. New Data on Why," *Psychology Today,* June 14, 2017, https://www.psychologytoday.com/us/blog/what-matters-most/201706/gen-z-strong-generation-new-data-why. Parker, Graf, and Igielnik.

40. "Generation Z Looks a Lot Like Millennials."

Chapter 2: Digital Everything: The Bad, The Ugly and The Good

41. "The Common Sense Census: Media Use by Tweens and Teens," Common Sense Media, 2019, https://www.commonsensemedia.org/research/the-common-sense-census-media-use-by-tweens-and-teens-2019.

42. J. M. Twenge, G. N. Martin, and W. K. Campbell, "Decreases in Psychological Well-Being among American Adolescents after 2012 and Links to Screen Time during the Rise of Smartphone Technology," *Emotion* 18, no. 6 (2018): 765–780, doi:10.1037/emo0000403.

43. Monica Anderson, "A Majority of Teens Have Experienced Some Form of Cyberbullying," Pew Research Center, September 27, 2018, https://www.pewinternet.org/2018/09/27/a-majority-of-teens-have-experienced-some-form-of-cyberbullying/#fn-21353-1.

44. A. J. Willingham, "The Family of a Teen Who Died by Suicide after Being Outed by Cyberbullies Is Demanding Justice," CNN, September 30, 2019, https://www.cnn.com/2019/09/30/us/channing-smith-suicide-cyberbullying-tennessee-trnd/index.html.

45. Elizabeth Chuck, "Bullying Drove 13-Year-Old Rosalie Avila to Kill Herself, Parents Say," NBC, December 5, 2017, https://www.nbcnews.com/news/us-news/bullying-drove-13-year-old-rosalie-avila-kill-herself-parents-n826281.

46. "Facts about Bullying," stopbullying.gov, https://www.stopbullying.gov/resources/facts.

47. Tristan Harris, "How Do You Ethically Steer the Thoughts and Actions of Two Billion People's Minds Every Day?" http://www.tristanharris.com/.

48. Anderson Cooper, "What Is 'Brain Hacking'? Tech Insiders on Why You Should Care," *60 Minutes,* CBS News, April 7, 2017, https://www.cbsnews.com/news/what-is-brain-hacking-tech-insiders-on-why-you-should-care/. Reprinted with permission of CBS News.

49. Andrew K. Przybylski and Netta Weinstein, "A Large-Scale Test of the Goldilocks Hypothesis: Quantifying the Relations Between Digital-Screen Use and the Mental Well-Being of Adolescents," *Psychological Science* 28, no. 2 (2017): 204–215, https://doi.org/10.1177/0956797616678438, Reprinted by Permission of SAGE Publications.

Chapter 3: The End of Youth as We Know It

50. Jean Twenge, "Why Today's Teens Aren't in Any Hurry to Grow Up," *The Conversation,* September 19, 2017, https://theconversation.com/why-todays-teens-arent-in-any-hurry-to-grow-up-83920.

51. Centers for Disease Control, "Youth Risk Behavior Survey (YRBS)," 2019, https://www.cdc.gov/healthyyouth/data/yrbs/index.htm.

52. National Center for Health Statistics, "Teen Births among Females Aged 15–19 Years, by Race and Hispanic Origin: United States, 2007–2017," Centers for Disease Control, https://www.cdc.gov/nchs/data/hus/2018/fig05.pdf.

53. Melissa S. Kearney and Phillip B. Levine, "Media Influences on Social Outcomes: The Impact of MTV's *16 and Pregnant* on Teen Childbearing," National Bureau of Economic Research Working Paper 19795, January 2014, Revised August 2015 JEL No. J13, L82.

54. Jennifer Manlove and Hannah Lantos, "Data Point: Half of 20- to 29-Year-Old Women Who Gave Birth in Their Teens Have a High School Diploma," *Child Trends,* January 11, 2018, https://www.childtrends.org/half-20-29-year-old-women-gave-birth-teens-high-school-diploma.

55. D. Finkelhor, "Are Kids Getting More Virtuous?" *Washington Post,* November 26, 2014, https://www.washingtonpost.com/opinions/the-kids-are-all-right-after-all/2014/11/26/63b9e494-70fe-11e4-8808-afaa1e3a33ef_story.html.

56. S. C. Curtin and M. Heron, "Death Rates Due to Suicide and Homicide among Persons Aged 10–24: United States, 2000–2017," *NCHS Data Brief* 352 (October 2019): 1–8.

57. Blue Cross Blue Shield, "Major Depression: The Impact on Overall Health," May 2018, https://www.bcbs.com/the-health-of-america/reports/major-depression-the-impact-overall-health.

58. Center for Collegiate Mental Health, "2018 Annual Report," Publication No. STA 19-180, January 2019, https://sites.psu.edu/ccmh/files/2019/09/2018-Annual-Report-9.27.19-FINAL.pdf.

59. Cigna, "Cigna 2018 U.S. Loneliness Index," https://www.cigna.com/static/www-cigna-com/docs/about-us/newsroom/studies-and-reports/combatting-loneliness/loneliness-survey-2018-full-report.pdf.

60. Jean M. Twenge, *IGen: Why Today's Super-Connected Kids Are Growing Up Less Rebellious, More Tolerant, Less Happy—and Completely Unprepared for Adulthood (And What That Means for the Rest of Us)* (New York: Atria, 2018), 104–116.

61. American Psychological Association, "Stress in America™, November 2019, https://www.apa.org/news/press/releases/stress/2019/stress-america-2019.pdf.

Chapter 4: Culture—Redefined

62. Nielsen Music, Year End Report, US 2019.

63. Brendan Klinkenberg, "Billboard May Revisit Decision to Remove 'Old Town Road' From Country Chart," *Rolling Stone,* April 6, 2019, https://www.rollingstone.com/music/music-news/lil-nas-x-old-town-road-billboard-country-chart-818635/.

64. Julia Pimentel, Carolyn Bernucca, Khal, Kevin L. Clark, and Manseen Logan, "Young Activists Who Are Changing the World," *Complex,* November 17, 2020, https://www.complex.com/life/young-activists-who-are-changing-the-world/.

65. *Juliana v. United States,* Wikipedia, https://en.wikipedia.org/wiki/Juliana_v._United_States.

66. "2019 Year in Swipe," Tinder, December 5, 2019: https://www.tinderpressroom.com/tinders-2019-year-in-swipe-r.

67. Laura Stavropoulos, "How Billie Eilish Went from Bedroom Musician to Global Icon in 8 Steps," *Discover Music,* March 28, 2020, https://www.udiscovermusic.com/stories/billie-eilish-introduction/amp/.

68. Gene Kosowan, "Billie Eilish's 10 Biggest Musical Influences, Ranked," TheTalko.com, July 5, 2020, https://www.thetalko.com/billie-eilish-music-influences-ranked/.

69. John Jurgensen, "Coming Soon to a Small Screen Near You: Short Cuts," *Wall Street Journal,* August 31, 2019, https://www.wsj.com/articles/coming-soon-to-a-small-screen-near-you-short-cuts-11567224030. Reprinted with permission WSJ Copyright © (2019) Dow Jones & Company, Inc. All Rights Reserved Worldwide. License number 4837780066987.

Chapter 5: Most Educated, Least Prepared?

70. S. Torn, "Top 10 Most Perfect and Relatable *Booksmart* Quotes," *Screen Rant,* June 14, 2019, https://screenrant.com/booksmart-quotes-perfect-relatable/.

71. World Economic Forum, "The Future of Jobs: Employment, Skills, and Workforce Strategy for the Fourth Industrial Revolution," January 2016, http://www3.weforum.org/docs/WEF_Future_of Jobs.pdf.

72. U.S. Census Bureau, "Table A-5b. Population 18 and 19 Years Old by School Enrollment Status, Sex, Race, and Hispanic Origin: October 1967 to 2017," https://www.census.gov/data/tables/time-series/demo/school-enrollment/cps-historical-time-series.html.

73. Richard Fry and Kim Parker, "Early Benchmarks Show 'Post-Millennials' on Track to Be Most Diverse, Best-Educated Generation Yet," Pew Research Center, November 2018, https://www.pewresearch.org/social-trends/2018/11/15/early-benchmarks-show-post-millennials-on-track-to-be-most-diverse-best-educated-generation-yet/.

74. Jeffrey J. Selingo, "College Students Say They Want a Degree for a Job. Are They Getting What They Want?" The Washington Post ©, September 1, 2018. All rights reserved. Used under license. https://www.washingtonpost.com/news/grade-point/wp/2018/09/01/college-students-say-they-want-a-degree-for-a-job-are-they-getting-what-they-want/.

75. Selingo, "College Students Say They Want a Degree for a Job."

76. U.S. Department of Education, National Center for Education Statistics, Higher Education General Information, Table 322.10, "Bachelor's degrees conferred by postsecondary institutions, by field of study, 2018," https://nces.ed.gov/programs/digest/d18/tables/dt18_322.10.asp.

77. Klaus Schwab, "The Fourth Industrial Revolution: What It Means, How to Respond," World Economic Forum, January 14, 2016, https://www.weforum.org/agenda/2016/01/the-fourth-industrial-revolution-what-it-means-and-how-to-respond.

78. A. Gray, "The 10 Skills You Need to Thrive in the Fourth Industrial Revolution," World Economic Forum, January 19, 2016, https://www.weforum.org/agenda/2016/01/the-10-skills-you-need-to-thrive-in-the-fourth-industrial-revolution/.

79. J. Puckett, Ernesto Pagano, Tyce Henry, Tobias Krause, Pashmeena Hilal, Arianna Trainito, and Abigail Frost, "Call for a New Era of Higher Ed–Employer Collaboration," July 7, 2020, The Boston Consulting Group, https://www.bcg.com/en-us/publications/2020/new-era-higher-ed-employer-collaboration.

80. Union College, "Academic Programs," https://www.union.edu/academic/majors-minors.

81. See the Iowa BIG website, https://iowabig.org/.

82. "15 More Companies That No Longer Require a Degree," Glassdoor, January 10, 2020, https://www.glassdoor.com/blog/no-degree-required/.

Chapter 6: Gen Z Employees—A World of Opposites

83. Russell Heimlich, "Baby Boomers Retire," Pew Research Center, December 29, 2010, https://www.pewresearch.org/fact-tank/2010/12/29/baby-boomers-retire/.

84. U.S. Bureau of Labor Statistics, "A Look at the Future of the U.S. Labor Force to 2060," Table 9: Distribution of Labor Force by Age, https://www.bls.gov/spotlight/2016/a-look-at-the-future-of-the-us-labor-force-to-2060/home.htm.

85. Dell Technologies, "Gen Z: The Future Has Arrived," 2018, https://www.delltechnologies.com/en-us/collaterals/unauth/sales-documents/solutions/gen-z-the-future-has-arrived-executive-summary.pdf.

86. Dell Technologies, "Gen Z."

87. Yello, "The 2019 Yello Recruiting Study: Meet Generation Z," 2019, https://yello.co/resource/white-paper/generation-z-recruiting-study/.

88. Yello, "2019 Yello Recruiting Study."

89. iCIMS, "The Class of 2019 Report," 2019, https://www.icims.com/resources/insights/. Glen this is the new 88.

90. "4 Companies Creatively Disrupting Social Recruiting," Jobologies, June 5, 2019, https://www.jobologies.com/4-companies-creatively-disrupting-social-recruiting/.

91. McDonald's, "McDonald's Restaurants Expect to Hire 250,000 People this Summer," June 12, 2017, https://news.mcdonalds.com/stories/our-people-details/mcdonalds-restaurants-expect-hire-250000-people-summer.

92. A. Moon and T. Mzezewa, "Goldman Sachs Taps Snapchat for Recruiting Millennials," September 18, 2015, https://www.reuters.com/article/us-goldman-sachs-snapchat-idUSKCN0RI2A620150918.

93. D. Rhatigan, “The Cultural Phenomenon of Emoji,” *Slideshare,* July 17, 2019, https://www.slideshare.net/adobe/adobe-emoji-trend-report-2019/1.

94. e-mail Interview with TechSmith, August 13, 2019.

95. e-mail Interview with TechSmith.

96. e-mail Interview with TechSmith.

97. Robert Half, “Get Ready for Generation Z,” August 1, 2015, https://www.roberthalf.com/blog/the-future-of-work/get-ready-for-generation-z.

98. “Move Over, Millennials: What You'll Need to Know for Hiring as Gen Z Enters the Workforce,” Monster.com, 2016, https://hiring.monster.com/litereg/genzreport.aspx.

99. “Move Over, Millennials.”

100. K. Ashley, “How Gen Z Influences Your Office Design,” Cushman Wakefield, July 15, 2019, https://www.cushmanwakefield.com/en/united-states/insights/us-articles/2019-07-atl-how-gen-z-influences-your-office-design.

101. Workforce Institute, “Meet Gen Z: The Next Generation Is Here: Hopeful, Anxious, Hardworking, and Searching for Inspiration,” 2019, https://workforceinstitute.org/wp-content/uploads/2019/05/Meet-Gen-Z-Hopeful-Anxious-Hardworking-and-Searching-for-Inspiration.pdf.

102. Door of Clubs, “What 5,000 Gen Z'ers Tell Us about the Future of Work,” November 30, 2017, https://medium.com/@doorofclubs/what-5-000-gen-zers-tell-us-about-the-future-of-work-6dd00f796e8f.

103. “Get Taken Care of,” Salesforce website, https://www.salesforce.com/company/careers/#why-sf.

104. S. Goff-Dupont, “Volunteer Time Off: Giving Employees a Perk That Gives Back,” *Work Life,* September 4, 2018, https://www.atlassian.com/blog/teamwork/volunteer-time-off-smart-investment-for-employers.

105. Goff-Dupont, “Volunteer Time Off.”

106. T. O'Shaughnessy, “Reality Check: Exploring Unrealistic Undergraduate Salary Expectations,” *Clever,* June 6, 2019, https://listwithclever.com/real-estate-blog/college-student-salary-expectations-study/.

Chapter 7: A Multigenerational Workforce

107. Richard Fry, "Baby Boomers Are Staying in the Labor Force at Rates Not Seen in Generations for People Their Age," Pew Research Center, July 24, 2019, https://www.pewresearch.org/fact-tank/2019/07/24/baby-boomers-us-labor-force/.

108. Bureau of Labor Statistics, "Employment Projections 2019–2029," September 1, 2020, https://www.bls.gov/news.release/pdf/ecopro.pdf.

109. Gina Weber, "Millennials Expect Less and More: Workplace Writing for Today's Workforce," Technical Communication Capstone Course, 24, Minnesota State University at Mankato, 2018, https://cornerstone.lib.mnsu.edu/eng_tech_comm_capstone_course/24/.

110. Bureau of Labor Statistics, "Table 3: Employment Status of the Civilian Noninstitutional Population by Age, Sex, and Race," https://www.bls.gov/cps/cpsaat03.htm.

111. "The Common Characteristics of Generation X Professionals," *The Balance Careers,* https://www.thebalancecareers.com/common-characteristics-of-generation-x-professionals-2164682.

112. Richard Fry, "Millennials Are the Largest Generation in the U.S. Labor Force," Pew Research Center, April 11, 2018, https://www.pewresearch.org/fact-tank/2018/04/11/millennials-largest-generation-us-labor-force/.

113. Erin Sherwood, "Workplace Managers Anticipate Big Challenges as Generation Z Enters the Workplace," Advanced Learning Institute, January 26, 2018, https://www.aliconferences.com/workplace-managers-anticipate-big-challenges-generation-z-enters-workplace/.

114. Randstad Workmonitor, "Impact of a Multi-Generational Workforce," 2nd quarter report, 2018, https://workforceinsights.randstad.com/hr-research-reports-workmonitor-q22018.

115. Kathleen McCleary, "5 Must-Knows about Millennial Managers," *Parade,* April 7, 2016, https://parade.com/468360/kmccleary/5-must-knows-about-millennial-managers/.

116. Chris Blauth, Jack McDaniel, Craig Perrin, and Paul B. Perrin, "Age-Based Stereotypes: Silent Killer of Collaboration and Productivity," AchieveGlobal, July 2, 2012, https://www.slideshare.net/mbonterre/age-based-stereotypes-research-report-achieve-globalagebased-stereotypes-silent-killer-of-collaboration-and-productivity.

117. Blauth, McDaniel, Perrin, and Perrin, "Age-Based Stereotypes."

118. "Mere Exposure Effect," January 29, 2016, https://psychology.iresearchnet.com/social-psychology/social-influence/mere-exposure-effect/.

119. Madeleine Burry, "Companies That Offer Tuition Reimbursement Programs," *The Balance Careers,* July 17, 2020, https://www.thebalancecareers.com/companies-offer-tuition-reimbursement-4126637.

Chapter 8: A Rising (Purchasing) Power

120. U.S. Bureau of Labor Statistics, "Employment status of the civilian noninstitutional population by age, sex, and race," (Table 3), "Usual weekly earnings of employed full-time wage and salary workers by age, sex, race," Table A-1, "Usual weekly earnings of employed part-time wage and salary workers by age, sex, race, Table A-12, Gen Z Planet research and analysis, https://www.bls.gov/cps/tables.htm.

121. National Retail Federation, "Keeping Up with Gen Z," October 1, 2019, https://nrf.com/research/consumer-view-fall-2019.

122. Mrinalini Krishna, "Millennials Are Risk Averse and Hoarding Cash," Investopedia, June 25, 2019, https://www.investopedia.com/news/millennials-are-risk-averse-and-hoarding-cash/.

123. Federal Reserve Bank, "Report on the Economic Well-Being of U.S. Households in 2018," May 2019, https://www.federalreserve.gov/publications/2019-economic-well-being-of-us-households-in-2018-preface.htm.

124. TransUnion, "As Gen Z Comes of Age, Credit Market Activity Shows Significant Growth," August 14, 2019, https://newsroom.transunion.com/as-gen-z-comes-of-age-credit-market-activity-shows-significant-growth/.

125. Bank of America, "Gen Z Got the Memo: Owning a Home Is Worth It," April 11, 2019, https://newsroom.bankofamerica.com/press-releases/consumer-banking/gen-z-got-memo-owning-home-worth-it.

126. See the Acorns website, https://www.acorns.com/about/.

127. The NPD Group, "Gen Zs Are Getting Older and Making Their Mark on Restaurants and Eating Trends," February 21, 2019, https://www.npd.com/wps/portal/npd/us/news/press-releases/2019/gen-zs-are-getting-older-and-making-their-mark-on-restaurants-and-eating-trends/.

Chapter 9: Gen Z Consumers—Accelerating Disruption

128. aerie, "Intimates Line aerie Gets Real, Unveils 'aerie Real' Spring 2014 Campaign Featuring Unretouched Models, Challenging Supermodel Standards," *Cision,* January 17, 2014, https://www.prnewswire.com/news-releases/intimates-line-aerie-gets-real-unveils-aerie-real-spring-2014-campaign-featuring-unretouched-models-challenging-supermodel-standards-240777281.html.

129. American Eagle Outfitters, "American Eagle Outfitters Reports Record Third Quarter Revenue," press release, December 11, 2019, http://investors.ae.com/news-releases/news-releases-details/2019/American-Eagle-Outfitters-Reports-Record-Third-Quarter-Revenue/default.aspx.

130. See the Hallmark website, https://corporate.hallmark.com/about/hallmark-cards-company/.

131. Hana Ben-Shabat, "Think Tank: Addressing the Consumer 'Trust Crisis,'" *WWD,* June 22, 2017, https://wwd.com/business-news/business-features/think-tank-influencers-beauty-10924192/.

132. Takumi, "Trust, Transactions, and Trend-Setters: The Realities of Influencer Marketing," August 2019.

133. See the Billie website, https://mybillie.com/.

134. "P&G Announces Plans to Acquire Billie Inc.," *BusinessWire,* January 8, 2020, https://www.businesswire.com/news/home/20200108005827/en/PG-Announces-Plans-Acquire-Billie.

135. Hana Ben-Shabat, "Gen Z and the Paradox of Luxury," *The Robin Report,* July 24, 2017, https://www.therobinreport.com/gen-z-and-the-paradox-of-luxury/.

136. Pew Research Center, "Teens' Social Media Habits and Experiences," November 28, 2018, https://www.pewresearch.org/internet/2018/11/28/teens-social-media-habits-and-experiences/.

137. Edelman, "Brands Make a Stand," October 2, 2018, https://www.edelman.com/earned-brand.

Chapter 10: Next-Generation Marketing

138. Lucy Tesseras, "Unilever CEO Says Keith Weed's Replacement Will Be a 'CMO++,'" *Marketing Week,* June 19, 2019, https://www.marketingweek.com/unilever-keith-weeds-replacement-cmo/.

139. Abha Bhattarai, "Levi Strauss CEO Takes a Side on Gun Control: 'It's Inevitable That We're Going to Alienate Some Consumers,'" *Washington Post,* September 10, 2018, https://www.washingtonpost.com/business/2018/09/10/levi-strauss-ceo-takes-side-gun-control-its-inevitable-that-were-going-alienate-some-consumers/.

140. K. C. Claveria, "Ungendered: Why Forward-Thinking Marketers Are Embracing Gender Fluidity," *Business2Community,* October 28, 2016, https://www.business2community.com/marketing/ungendered-forward-thinking-marketers-embracing-gender-fluidity-01688037.

141. "Makeup Brand Glossier Valued at Over $1 Billion in Latest Funding Round," Reuters, March 19, 2019, https://www.reuters.com/article/us-glossier-funding/makeup-brand-glossier-valued-at-over-1-billion-in-latest-funding-round-idUSKCN1R01KW.

142. Peter Kafka, "Food52, the Recipes + Cookware Site Founded by a Former New York Times Food Columnist, Is Gobbled Up," September 29, 2019, https://www.vox.com/recode/2019/9/29/20889854/food52-chernin-amanda-hesser.

143. National Retail Federation and IBM Institute for Business Value, "Gen Z Brand Relationships," IBM, July 2017.

144. Amanda DeFelice, "From Rags to Riches: Daniel Wellington," Fox School of Business, Temple University, November 10, 2019, https://digitalmarketing.temple.edu/adefelice/2019/11/10/from-rags-to-riches-daniel-wellington/.

145. See the Unidays website, https://www.myunidays.com/US/en-US/content/nastygaldesigner-closed.

146. Kurt Schroeder, "Why So Many New Products Fail (and It's Not the Product)," *The Business Journals,* March 17, 2017, https://www.bizjournals.com/bizjournals/how-to/marketing/2017/03/why-so-many-new-products-fail-and-it-s-not-the.html.

147. Matt Ariker, Alejandro Díaz, Jason Heller, and Jesko Perrey, "Personalizing at Scale," McKinsey & Co., November 1, 2015, https://www.mckinsey.com/business-functions/marketing-and-sales/our-insights/personalizing-at-scale.

148. Charity Stebbins, "Educational Content Makes Consumers 131% More Likely to Buy," *Spotlight Conductor,* July 6, 2017, https://www.conductor.com/blog/2017/07/winning-customers-educational-content/.

149. See the Yummly website, https://www.yummly.com/.

150. Stephen Kim, "JetBlue—The Ultimate Icebreaker," *Bizzabo,* July 19, 2017, https://blog.bizzabo.com/experiential-marketing-examples#jetblue.

151. Desperados, "Epic Parties—Charging Wall," YouTube, April 1, 2019, https://www.youtube.com/watch?v=hYUMZkQC1Y4.

Index

List of Figures and Tables

List of Illustrations

About the Author

HANA BEN-SHABAT IS the founder of Gen Z Planet, a research and advisory firm helping leaders across sectors and industries to prepare for the next generation of culture creators, employees, and consumers.

Known for her creativity, expertise, and insights, Hana is an award-winning management consultant who was named as one of the "Top 25 Consultants" by *Consulting Magazine* for her thought leadership in retail. She is a sought-after speaker and commentator on consumer behaviors and trends, and over the years she has been quoted in leading media publications such as The Wall Street Journal, New York Times, San Francisco Chronicle, The Economist, Forbes and Fortune as well as Women's Wear Daily and Business of Fashion.

Before founding Gen Z Planet, Hana was a partner and board member of the global management consulting firm Kearney where she co-led the firm's Global Consumer Institute and advised clients around the world on issues of corporate strategy and organizational effectiveness. Before that she held marketing positions at several Israeli tech companies.

Hana is a graduate of the David Rockefeller fellowship, a leadership program designed to facilitate public-private partnerships. She is a member of the expert network of New York Fashion Tech Lab where she mentors women founders, and she serves as an advisor and board member of several startups at the intersection of technology and consumer products.

Hana holds a B.A. degree in Political Science (major) and Psychology (minor) from Tel Aviv University, an M.B.A from Rotterdam School of Management, and a diploma in Corporate Finance from the London Business School.

To learn more about Gen Z Planet's research, speaking engagements and advisory services please visit www.genzplanet.com